CW00555782

TRADITIONAL TURKISH SAVOURY
DISHES CAKES AND DESSERTS

Esen Hengirmen

ISBN 975 - 320 - 012 - 9

Text	: Esen HENGİRMEN
Photos	: Dr. Mehmet HENGİRMEN
General Director	: Serap YASA
Translator	: Ahu GÖKDEMİR
Graphic Designer	: Serap YASA
Reductor	: Christine TEKİN
Typesetter	: Mualla EDEN

Published by © Engin Yayınevi, 1997
Selanik Caddesi 28 / 6
Kızılay 06 650 ANKARA
Telefon : (312) 419 49 20
(312) 419 49 21
Faks : (312) 419 49 22

Printed by Ekip Grafik - ANKARA
(312) 341 65 56

CONTENTS

Soups

RED LENTIL SOUP (Serves 6)
KIRMIZI MERCİMEK ÇORBASI

INGREDIENTS

1 glass of red lentils

8 glasses of meat stock or water

1 medium sized onion(grated)

1 medium sized potato

1 medium sized carrot

1 tblsp. butter

1 glass of milk

1 egg - yolk

2 cloves of garlic

1 tblsp. tomato paste

salt, pepper , dried mint

COOKING

❧ Melt the butter in a saucepan. Fry the grated onion until golden brown.

❧ Add washed lentils, grated potato, carrot, garlic, tomato paste and pepper.

❧ Add 8 glasses of stock or water and boil it until tender then strain through a sieve.

❧ Mix egg - yolk and milk, stirring well. Add the mixture to the soup 5 minutes before ready to serve. Cook 1-2 minutes more. Before serving add salt.

❧ Prepare a hot sauce by heating mint, pepper and oil, then pour over the soup.

2

DAWN SOUP (Serves 6)
ŞAFAK ÇORBASI

INGREDIENTS
8 glasses of meat stock
3 tbsps. flour
3 tbsps. butter
5-6 tomatoes or
2 tbsps. tomato paste
1 glass of milk
2 egg - yolks
salt

COOKING

❦ Melt the butter in a saucepan and fry the flour in it until golden brown.

❦ Add peeled tomatoes or the tomato paste and mix for 1-2 minutes,
  Add the stock.

❦ Simmer until the tomatoes are soft then strain through a sieve.

❦ Boil for a further 1-2 minutes.

❦ Beat the egg - yolks and add milk. Beat a little more then stir the
  mixture into the soup 20 minutes before ready to serve.
  Before serving add salt.

TRIPE SOUP WITH EGG SAUCE
(Serves 6)
TERBİYELİ İŞKEMBE ÇORBA

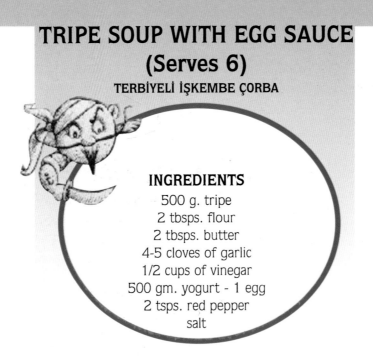

INGREDIENTS
500 g. tripe
2 tbsps. flour
2 tbsps. butter
4-5 cloves of garlic
1/2 cups of vinegar
500 gm. yogurt - 1 egg
2 tsps. red pepper
salt

COOKING

- Boil the well cleaned and washed tripe in salty water and chop it up.
- Beat the flour, egg and yogurt in a deep pan. Add the chopped tripe together with its juice. Boil it for 10 minutes more and add salt.
- Serve it with crushed garlic and vinegar.

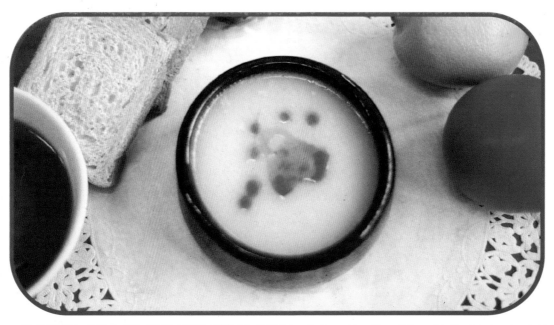

TOMATO SOUP (Serves 6)

DOMATES ÇORBASI

INGREDIENTS

1,5 litres meat stock or water
2 tbsps. flour
2 tbsps. butter
500 g. ripe red tomatoes or
2 tbsps. tomato paste
1 glass of milk
1 egg - yolk
1 tsp. black pepper

COOKING

❧ Melt the butter, gradually add flour, stir over the heat for 1-2 minutes.
❧ Add grated tomatoes or tomato paste. Gradually add the meat stock, stir well until it boils.
❧ Beat the milk and egg-yolk. Add to the soup 10 minutes before serving and add salt.
❧ Garnish with croutons (fried bread cubes).

YOGURT AND MINT SOUP
(Serves 6)

YAYLA ÇORBASI

INGREDIENTS

10 glasses of meat stock

1/2 glass of rice

1 tbsp. flour

2 glasses of yogurt

1 egg

1 tbsp. butter

1 tsp. dried mint, red pepper, salt.

COOKING

- ❦ Put the washed rice and meat stock in a saucepan. Simmer until the rice is very tender.
- ❦ Mix the flour, egg, and yogurt in a separate bowl. Then pour it into the soup.
- ❦ Boil for 10 minutes more stirring thoroughly. Before serving add salt.
- ❦ Pour hot pepper sauce over on serving. (Heated oil, pepper and dried mint)

MUSHROOM SOUP
(Serves 5)
MANTAR ÇORBASI

INGREDIENTS
250 g. mushrooms
2 litres of meat stock
1 glass of milk
1 small glass of flour
1 tbsp. butter
juice of 1 lemon
salt

COOKING
- Wash the mushrooms by rubbing them well. Let them wait in a separate bowl with lemon juice for a while then chop them up.
- In a deep pan, melt the butter and fry mushrooms . Add meat stock and boil.
- Beat the flour and milk in another bowl. Pour this gradually into the soup, add salt. Cook for a further 30 minutes before serving.

CAULIFLOWER SOUP (Serves 5)

KARNIBAHAR ÇORBASI

INGREDIENTS

1 small cauliflower
5 glasses of meat stock
1 glass of milk
1/2 cup of flour
1 tbsp. butter
1 small onion
1 medium sized leek (white part)
1 small clery
salt

COOKING

- Cut the head of cauliflower into sections, then wash and boil them. Separate the florets and stalks. Put the florets into a deep pan.
- Melt the butter in a separate deep pan. Add chopped onion, leek, celery, salt and meat stock. Then boil them altogether.
- Meanwhile in a separate bowl, mix the flour in the milk and gradually add it to the soup, stirring well. Season and simmer for a further 30 minutes. Strain through a sieve.
- Add the florets of cauliflower to the strained soup then boil it for a further 1-2 minutes. Serve.

VERMICELLI SOUP WITH EGG SAUCE (Serves 5)
TERBİYELİ ŞEHRİYE ÇORBA

INGREDIENTS
7-8 glasses of meat stock
2 cups of vermicelli
3 eggs
juice of 1/2 lemon
1 tblsp. butter
salt, black pepper

COOKING
❦ Bring meat stock and salt to boil in a large pan.
❦ Toss the vermicelli into the boiling stock. Cook for a further 30 minutes.
❦ Beat the eggs with lemon juice, add a glass of water.
❦ Pour the mixture gradually into the boiling soup. Boil for a further minute, stirring well. Before it is ready to serve, pour over a sauce made with the melted butter and red pepper.

SOUP WITH MEATBALLS AND YOGURT (Serves 5)

KÖFTELİ YOĞURTLU ÇORBA

INGREDIENTS

200 g. minced lamb

1/2 cup of uncooked rice

2 tbsps. flour

2 eggs

salt, black pepper

500 g. yogurt

1 tbsp. butter

1 tbsp. driedmint

1 tsp. red pepper

1/4 bunch of parsley
(chopped)

7-8 glasses of meat stock

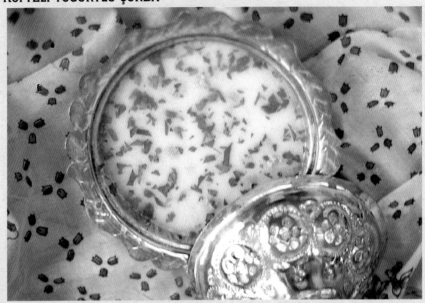

COOKING

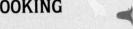

- ❦ Boil the meat stock together with rice and salt in a saucepan.
- ❦ Mix the minced lamb, salt, pepper and parsley together. Wetting the palms with a little water each time, break off small walnut - sized pieces of the mixture and form them into balls.
- ❦ Place the balls into a shallow pan containing the flour and shake it to coat them with flour.
- ❦ Pour 2-3 glasses of hot water over the balls and let them stand for 5 minutes.
- ❦ Strain the balls and add them to the boiling water and rice. Cook until the rice is very tender.
- ❦ Beat the eggs, yogurt and flour in a separate bowl. Dilute this with a glass of water then add to the soup.
- ❦ Add the mint and boil it for a further 5 minutes. Before serving, melt the butter and stir in 2 teaspoons of red pepper. Pour onto the soup when serving.

FISH SOUP (Serves 6)

BALIK ÇORBASI

INGREDIENTS

1 large lesser grey mullet
1 cup of oil
1 medium sized carrot
1 small celery
1 bunch of parsley
1 clove of garlic

2 medium sized onions
1/2 glass uncooked rice
juice of 1 lemon
3 eggs
black pepper, salt
2 bay leaves

COOKING

❧ Gut and clean the fish, then cut into pieces.

❧ Boil 12-13 glasses of water in a saucepan with half of chopped celery and carrot, onion, salt, black pepper and bay-leaves. Boil for an hour. Strain through a sieve.

❧ Chop the rest of the celery and carrot into thin pieces. Chop the other halves of onion and parsley too. Fry them in oil in a deep pan. Add crushed garlic, parsley, strained fish sauce, salt and rice. Cook until the rice is very tender.

❧ Beat the eggs with lemon juice in a separate bowl. First dilute it with a glass of water then stir into the soup. Cook it 5 minutes more before serving. Garnish with chopped parsley.

INGREDIENTS

8-9 glasses of meat stock

3 tbsps. flour

1 egg

4-5 onions

2 cups of grated cheese

1 glass of milk

2 tbsps. butter

salt

18

ONION SOUP
SOĞAN ÇORBA

COOKING
(Serves 5)

- Chop the onions in rings and fry in butter in a deep pan. Add the flour and stir it for a further 1-2 minutes then pour in the meat stock together with the salt. Stir well until it boils. Cook 30 minutes more. Strain through a sieve.

- After straining, boil the soup in another saucepan.

- Beat the egg and milk in another bowl and pour it gradually into the soup, stirring well. Boil for a further 5 minutes. Then change the pan with an ovenproof pan. Add the grated cheese then put it into the oven. Let it cook until golden brown.

Vegetable Dishes

STUFFED VEGETABLES WITH MEAT
(Serves 10)
ETLİ DOLMALAR

INGREDIENTS

Stuffed green peppers, aubergines, courgettes, tomatoes ; 1 kg.
vine - leaves; 1/2 kg.
cabbage leaves; 2 kg.
500 g. minced lamb (low in fat)
1 cup of uncooked rice
2 medium sized onions
2 tbsp. tomato paste
1/2 bunch of parsley and of dill
1 tbsp. dried mint
3 cloves of garlic
2 tbsps. butter
juice of 1 lemon
salt, black pepper, red pepper

COOKING

❧ Cut off a small lid from the top of the peppers, then cut out the seeds and veins.
❧ Peel alternate lengthwise (finger wide) strips from the aubergines. Then cut in half widthwise. Hollow out the centre of each.
❧ Cut off a small lid from the top of the tomatoes and hollow out the seeds and core.
❧ Wash and drain.
❧ Toss vine - and - cabbage leaves into boiling water until they become softer.
❧ Stuffing: Mix minced lamb, chopped onions, garlic, parsley, dill, mint, salt and black pepper and add butter.
❧ Add rice, half glass of water, lemon juice and knead them all. Then stuff the vegetables with the mixture and cover each with a tomato lid before arranging them in a saucepan.
❧ Pour over 3 glasses of tomato paste mixed with water, juice of 1/2 lemon and 1 tbsp. butter, cook it until the rice is tender.

STUFFED VEGETABLES IN OLIVE OIL(Serves 10)

ZEYTİNYAĞLI DOLMALAR

INGREDIENTS
green peppers,
aubergines; 1 kg
cabbage-leaves; 2 kg
vine-leaves; 1/2 kg
1/2 tbsp tomato paste
500 g. uncooked rice
1/2 kg. onions
1,5 glasses of olive oil
2 tbsp. of pine nuts
2 tbsp. of currants
1/2 bunch of parsley
and of dill
1 tbsp. of dried mint
1 lemon
1 tsp. black pepper
        paprika,
        cinammon,
        salt

COOKING

- 🐚 In a deep pan chop the onions and sauté in the olive oil with pine nuts until tender.
- 🐚 Pick over and wash the rice and stir well with 1/2 tomato paste for 1-2 seconds.
- 🐚 Add some water to cover the rice, cook it with its lid on till the rice absorbs the water.
- 🐚 Let it rest for 5-10 minutes.
- 🐚 Add chopped dill, parsley, driedmint, currants, cinammon, paprika, salt, black pepper and lemon juice. Stir them all well.
- 🐚 Stuff or roll up the vegetables around the mixture. Arrange them in a saucepan. Add 3 glasses of hot water. Cook until the rice absorbs the water.
- 🐚 Set aside to cool.
- 🐚 Garnish with slices of lemon and parsley
- 🐚 Serve cold.

VEGETABLE DISHES WITH MEAT (Serves 10)
ETLİ TAZE SEBZELER

INGREDIENTS
1 kg. vegetables
(Beans, Peas, Okra)
500 g. cubed meat
2 tbsps. butter
2 medium sized onions
1 medium sized tomato
1 tbsp. tomato paste
2 long green peppers
salt
1 tsp. black pepper

COOKING
❦ Chop the onions and brown in a saucepan with butter and cubed meat.
❦ Add chopped tomato or tomato paste.
❦ Add 3 glasses of water and cook until the meat is tender.
❦ Add the stringed and sliced vegetables. Cook with lid on for a further 10 minutes.
❦ Add some water (but do not let the water cover the vegetables) simmer for 10 minutes until the vegetables are tender.
❦ Add salt to taste before it is ready to serve.

AUBERGINES STUFFED WITH MEAT (Serves 6)

PATLICAN KARNIYARIK

INGREDIENTS
300 g. minced lamb
6 medium sized aubergines
2 medium sized onions
3 green peppers
3 tomatoes
1/2 bunch of parsley
4 tbsps. of butter
salt, black pepper

COOKING

- Cut off the stalks of the aubergines and peel alternate lengthwise strips. Stand in salty water for 30 minutes. Wash and dry well.
- Fry in butter and arrange in rows in a shallow cooking pan. Cut the middles lengthwise.
- Fry the chopped onions, pepper and minced lamb in the remaining butter. Add peeled and chopped tomatoes, chopped parsley, salt, and pepper, stir well.
- Stuff the aubergines with the mixture. Cover them with sliced tomato halves.
- Add only a little water. Cook in oven or over a low heat for 15 or 20 minutes.
- Serve hot.

CASSEROLED AUBERGINE (Serves 10)
PATLICAN GÜVEÇ

INGREDIENTS
750 g.lamb cut into cubes
5 medium sized aubergines
5 medium sized tomatoes
8 thin green peppers
1 large onion
1 bunch of garlic
2 tbsps. butter
salt and black pepper

COOKING
- Use an earthenware casserole.
- Put the cubed lamb into the casserole.
- Peel and cut the aubergines into small pieces. Then add to the meat
- Put chopped onions, garlic, pepper, tomotoes (cut into 4 pieces) over the aubergines.
- Add butter, salt and black pepper. Add water to half way up the vegetables. Cover with aluminium foil and then place it in the oven at 180°C.
- If the top is not golden brown, uncover the foil and let it cook until golden.

VEGETABLES IN OLIVE OIL (Serves 6)
ZEYTİNYAĞLI TAZE SEBZELER

INGREDIENTS
1/2 kg. vegetables
(beans, courgettes, leeks,
broad beans, jerusalem
artichokes, celery)
1/2 glass of olive oil
1 medium sized onion
1 medium sized tomato
1/2 tbsp. tomato paste
3/4 cloves of garlic
1 carrot
1 tsp. sugar
Salt

COOKING
* Wash and chop the vegetables.
* Sauté chopped onions, carrots and garlic in olive oil.
* Add chopped tomato and tomato paste.
* Stir in washed and chopped vegetables. Cook with the lid on, for a further 10 minutes.
* Add 2 glasses of hot water and cook until the vegetables are tender.
* Add salt 10 minutes before serving. This olive oil vegetable dish should have a little sauce.
* Set aside to cool.
* Garnish with parsley, mint and slices of lemon.
* Serve cold.

If courgette, leek or Jerusalem artichokes are being cooked, add a half cup of rice to the vegetables

P.S.Do not add tomato paste to Jerusalem artichokes.

AUBERGINES STUFFED WITH SWEETENED ONIONS (Serves 6)
PATLICAN İMAM BAYILDI

INGREDIENTS

6 medium sized
   aubergines
3 medium sized onions
3 green peppers
3 tomatoes
1 bunch of garlic
1/2 bunch of parsley
1 glass of olive oil
1 tsp. sugar
salt, black pepper

COOKING

- ❦ Peel lengthwise down both sides of each aubergine. Stand in salty water for 30 minutes. Then wash and dry.
- ❦ Fry them in olive oil until golden brown and arrange them in rows in a wide and shallow saucepan. Cut the middles length wise.
- ❦ Fry the chopped onions, pepper and garlic in the remaining oil. Add peeled and chopped tomatoes, chopped parsley, salt, pepper and sugar to the mixture. Stir well.
- ❦ Stuff the mixture into the whole aubergines and cover them with sliced tomato halves.
- ❦ Add only a little water. Cook in oven or over a low heat for 15 or 20 minutes.
- ❦ Serve lukewarm or cold.

ARTICHOKES WITH BROAD BEANS COOKED IN OLIVE OIL (Serves 6)

ZEYTİNYAĞLI İÇ BAKLALI ENGİNAR

INGREDIENTS

6 artichokes
1 carrot (diced)
1 medium sized potato
1/2 kg. fresh broad beans
1 large onion
150 g. olive oil
1 lemon
1/2 bunch of chopped dill
1 tsp. salt and sugar
1 tbsp. flour.
2 glasses of water

COOKING

❦ Remove the outer leaves, stems and purple chokes of artichokes. Put them into salty and floured water with half of the lemon juice.

❦ Put olive oil into a shallow saucepan, sauté the chopped onions, and carrot together. Add the juice of halfa lemon, 2 glasses of water, salt, sugar, artichokes, and broad beans. Put the lid on the saucepan and bring to the boil until the vegetables are tender.

❦ Arrange the cooked artichokes on a serving dish, fill them with the stuffing. Pour the sauce of the vegetables over it. Sprinkle chopped dill on top, then serve.

COURGETTE FRITTERS (Serves 6)
KABAK MÜCVERİ

INGREDIENTS

4 medium sized
   courgettes
1 medium sized onion
3-4 long green peppers
1/2 bunch of parsley
1/2 bunch of dill
4 eggs
4 tbsp. flour
salt, black pepper
1 glass of oil (for frying)

COOKING

❧ Wash, peel and grate the courgettes. Add chopped onion, pepper, chopped parsley, dill, salt, black pepper, eggs and flour. Mix thoroughly.

❧ Drop a tablespoonful at a time into hot oil and fry until golden brown on both sides.

❧ Drain on a piece of kitchen paper. Best served hot.

BAKED CAULIFLOWER CHEESE (Serves 10)

FIRINDA KARNIBAHAR

INGREDIENTS

1 large cauliflower
150 g. grated cheese
1/2 lt. milk
100 g. wheat flour
100 g. oil
salt, red and black pepper
3 eggs.

COOKING

❧ Wash and divide the cauliflower. Boil in salty water until tender, strain and divide the cauliflower into portion-sized florets.

❧ Fry the oil and flour in a saucepan until golden brown. Add milk gradually. Cook it for a further 1-2 minutes, then remove from heat and let it cool. Add salt, black and red pepper, and eggs. Stir well. Mix half of this mixture with cauliflower's florets.

❧ Place half of the mixture into an greased oven dish. Place the florets in the middle and pour the other half on top, pour over one spoon of melted butter. Sprinkle the grated cheese, then cook in oven until golden brown. Serve hot.

FRIED CAULIFLOWER-CARROTS (Serves 10)

KARNIBAHAR - HAVUÇ KIZARTMA

INGREDIENTS

4 large carrots or
1 kg. cauliflower
1 glass of olive oil
4 eggs
2 tbsps. of flour
salt

COOKING

❧ Boil cauliflower or carrots. Strain.

❧ Divide the cauliflower into florets and flatten in palm. For carrots cut them into slices. Beat the eggs and add gradually to the flour. Add a pinch of salt. Dip them in the mixture to coat then and fry in oil until golden brown.

EGG WITH MUSHROOMS
MANTARLI YUMURTA
(Serves 6)

INGREDIENTS

1 kg. fresh mushrooms

6 eggs

1 tbsp. butter

1 medium sized onion

salt and black pepper

COOKING

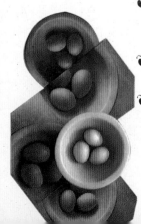

- ❦ Clean and wash the mushrooms well. Boil them without a lid for an hour. Add some cold water to make them warm. Take them out by rubbing in your palms. Then chop up.
- ❦ Melt butter in a saucepan. Fry the sliced mushrooms for 10 minutes, add salt and pepper. Place them into another saucepan.
- ❦ Poach the eggs over the mushrooms and cook it with the lid on until the whites are set but the yolks are runny.

POACHED EGGS WITH YOGURT
ÇILBIR
(Serves 6)

INGREDIENTS
6 eggs
2 glasses of yogurt
4 cloves of garlic
1 tblsp. butter
1/2 cup of vinegar
salt and black pepper

COOKING

❦ Boil some water in a shallow pan, add salt and vinegar. Poach the eggs. Boil until the whites are just cooked, but the yolks are still runny. Place into a serving dish.

❦ Pour over the yogurt which has had the crushed garlic mixed in.

❦ Melt the butter and after removing from the heat, sprinkle in red pepper. Pour the mixture over the eggs and yogurt.

AUBERGINE PURÉE (Serves 10)
HÜNKÂR BEĞENDİ

INGREDIENTS

Kebab	Aubergine Purée
1 kg. minced beef	5 aubergines
2 medium sized onions	1 tbsp. flour
3-4 tomatoes	2 tbsps. butter
2 tbsps. butter	1 glass of milk
salt, black pepper	3 tbsps. grated cheddar type cheese
	1/2 bunch of parsley
	salt and black pepper

COOKING

Kebab:

- Fry the chopped onions and minced beef in butter. Stir well with peeled and chopped tomatoes. Add 3 glasses of water, salt and pepper. Cook until the meat is tender. There should be a little liquid left.

Purée:

- Char the unpeeled aubergines over an open flame. Cut in half longways and scoop out the white centre.
- Meanwhile melt the butter in a saucepan and stir in the flour. Add chopped aubergines, grated cheese, milk and salt. Stir until well mixed.
- Put the purée into a large dish and put the kebab over it. Garnish it with parsley.

CHICK-PEA PURÉE
HUMUS

INGREDIENTS

1 glass of chick - peas

1/2 glass of tahin

(crushed sesame seeds)

1/2 glass of olive - oil

1/2 tbsp. of red pepper

5-6 cloves of garlic

juice of 3 lemons

salt

COOKING

❧ Soak chick - peas overnight in a saucepan full of salty water. Rinse and boil until they become tender. Remove the skins.

❧ Blend the chick - peas to a fine purée.

❧ Add tahin, crushed garlic, pepper and salt.

❧ Gradually pour olive oil and lemon juice while stirring / blending well.

❧ Spread in a shallow dish and garnish with pickles, olives, parsley and slices of lemon.

HIBESH PASTE
HİBEŞ

INGREDIENTS
1 glass of tahin
(crushed sesame seeds)
juice of 2 lemons
1 cup of olive oil
1/2 tbsp. cummin
4 cloves of garlic
1/2 tbsp. red pepper
1/2 bunch of chopped parsley
salt.

COOKING

❦ Put tahin, crushed garlic, cummin and pepper into a bowl and mix.

❦ Gradually add lemon juice, and olive oil. Add salt as the last step; stir well.

❦ Spread in a shallow dish and garnish with slices of lemon, pickles or parsley.

WALNUT PASTE

TARATOR

INGREDIENTS

1 glass of shelled walnuts
1/2 glass of tahin (crushed
　　sesame seeds)
　　juice of 1 lemon
3 cloves of garlic
2 tsps. red pepper
1/2 bunch of chopped parsley
　　salt

COOKING

❧ Mix crushed and shelled walnuts, garlic, tahin, lemon juice, salt, red pepper and chopped parsley in a bowl.

❧ Spread the mixture in a shallow dish and garnish it with pickles, and slices of lemon.

CAVIARE SAUCE

TARAMA

INGREDIENTS

100 g. caviare
3 slices of stale bread
    crumbs
1/2 glass of hot milk
1 glass of olive oil
1 tbsp. red pepper
Juice of 2 lemons
salt

COOKING

❧ Mix hot milk, bread crumbs, caviare, olive oil, lemon juice, salt and pepper in a bowl. Beat thoroughly.
❧ Spread the mixture in a shallow serving dish and garnish with lemon, pickles and parsley.

WHITE BEAN SALAD (Serves 6)

FASÜLYE PİYAZI

INGREDIENTS

1 glass of beans
3 hard boiled eggs
2 onions
1-2 tomatoes
5-6 long green peppers
15-20 olives
1/2 glass of olive oil
1/2 glass of vinegar
black and red pepper, salt

COOKING

- ❦ Soak the beans overnight. Rinse and boil them in water until tender. Then wash, strain and put them in a serving dish.
- ❦ Add sliced onions, pepper, parsley, salt, red and black pepper, chopped tomatoes and eggs. Mix them all well, then add olives.
- ❦ Sprinkle on olive oil and vinegar.
- ❦ Put into a serving dish and garnish.

POTATO SALAD (Serves 6)
PATATES SALATASI

INGREDIENTS

4 medium sized potatoes
1 medium sized onion
1/2 bunch of parsley
4-5 long green peppers
1 tomato
15-20 olives
1/2 glass of olive oil
1 lemon
salt - black and red pepper
1 tblsp. mint.

COOKING

❧ Boil the potatoes until tender. Peel and after cutting them into 4 pieces, thinly slice them.
❧ Add sliced onion, pepper, diced tomato, coarsely chopped parsley, mint, olives, salt, black and red pepper.
❧ Mix olive oil and lemon juice and pour over the mixture.
❧ Spread the mixture into a serving dish and garnish.

POTATO CROQUETTES (Serves 6)

PATATES KÖFTESİ

INGREDIENTS
4-5 potatoes
3 eggs
50 g. white Turkish cheese
1/2 bunch of parsley
salt, black pepper
3-4 tbsps. flour
1 glass of oil (for frying)

COOKING
- Boil the potatoes until they are tender then grate them when cold.
- Add 1 egg, grated cheese, chopped parsley, salt and black pepper.
- Take and form walnut-sized pieces.
- Beat the eggs in a separate bowl.
- First dip each ball into flour then into beaten eggs. Fry in hot oil until golden brown.
- Drain on a piece of kitchen paper then place in a serving dish.

AUBERGINE SALAD

PATLICAN SALATASI

(Serves 6)

INGREDIENTS
5 large aubergines
5-6 long green peppers
1 tomato
1 medium sized onion
1/2 bunch of parsley
1/3 glass of olive oil
juice of 1 lemon
salt, black and
red pepper

COOKING

- Char the aubergines over an open flame until they are soft. Cut lengthwise. Scoop out flesh and mash.
- Put the mashed aubergines into a bowl and add chopped parsley, pepper, tomato and onion.
- Add salt, black and red pepper, lemon juice and olive oil, beat well together.
- Place in a shallow serving dish and garnish.

CARROTS WITH YOGURT
YOĞURTLU HAVUÇ SALATASI

INGREDIENTS:

1/2 kg. carrot.
1/2 kg. yogurt
1/2 glass of olive oil
4-5 cloves of garlic
1/4 bunch of parsley
Salt

COOKING

- ❧ Peel and wash the carrots then coarsely grate them. Sauté in oil for 1-2 minutes.
- ❧ Cook over a low heat with lid on. Stir once or twice until lightly cooked.
- ❧ Crush the garlic with salt and add to yogurt.
- ❧ Add yogurt to the carrot purée and place into a serving dish.
- ❧ Garnish with parsley.

JAJIK (Serves 6)
(COLD YOGURT AND CUCUMBER SOUP- CACIK)

INGREDIENTS
500 g. yogurt
250 g. cucumber
250 cc. water
4-5 cloves of garlic
3 tbsps. olive oil
1 tbsp. mint or 1/2 bunch of dill
salt

COOKING
❦ Beat and crush garlic with salt.
❦ Mix yogurt, peeled and finely chopped cucumbers, crushed garlic, olive oil, mint or chopped dill together with salt.
❦ Add 250 cc water to bring it to the consistency of thick soup.
❦ Divide into bowls. Sprinkle a pinch of mint or chopped dill over.

RUSSIAN SALAD
RUS SALATASI

INGREDIENTS
3 medium sized boiled potatoes
2 medium sized boiled carrots
3/4 glasses of peas (tinned)
4-5 slices of salami
10-15 small gherkins
Mayonnaise:
1,5 glasses of olive oil
2 fresh egg-yolks
1 tsp. mustard powder
1 lemon
salt

COOKING

- Put egg-yolks, salt and mustard powder in a bowl.
- Beat while gradually pouring in olive oil. Gradually add lemon juice. (Leave aside 3 spoons of the mixture)
- Add little cube shaped chopped carrots, potatoes, gherkins, peas, and salami. Stir well.
- Place the mixture into a serving dish. Garnish with parsley and left over mayonnaise mixture.

Chicken, cooked or chopped celery, jerusalem artichokes, or cauliflower may be added into the mayonnaise.

Meat Dishes

MEATBALLS ON SKEWERS
ŞİŞ KÖFTE

INGREDIENTS

1/2 kg. minced lamb. (Moderately fatty)
Crumbs from 2 slices of bread
2 cloves of garlic
1 onion
chopped parsley (1 tbsp.)
salt, black pepper
1 egg.

COOKING

❦ The meat should be minced twice. Mix together the minced lamb, chopped onion, garlic, wetted and squeezed bread crumbs, chopped parsley, salt, black pepper and yogurt. Knead the mixture well.
Taking one egg-sized piece at a time into your palm, work it around the skewer, gradually squeezing lengthwise.
❦ Cook over charcoal barbecue, in oven or on grill.
❦ Cooked meatballs on skewers can be served with fried potatoes, barbecued long green peppers, tomatoes and onions.

47

EGG COATED MEATBALLS
KADIN BUDU KÖFTE

INGREDIENTS

1/2 kg. lean minced lamb
(moderately fatty)
2 onions
2 tbsp. rice
4 eggs
1 tbsp. chopped parsely
3-4 tbsp.stale bread crumbs-chop in
blender
salt, black pepper
1 glass of oil for frying (olive oil etc.)
1 tbsp. butter.

COOKING

- ❦ Melt the butter and sauté half of the minced lamb in it. Stir to prevent it forming lumps.
- ❦ Wash the rice and boil until it is tender then strain through a sieve.
- ❦ Into the cooked minced lamb, add the other half of the meat, boiled and strained rice, 2 eggs, chopped parsley, salt and black pepper. Mix well.
- ❦ Divide the mixture into egg-sized pieces and shape into ovals.
- ❦ Beat the remaining eggs. First dip each meat ball into bread crumbs then into egg mixture before frying in the hot oil until brown on both sides.
- ❦ Drain on a piece of kitchen paper before serving. Place onto a serving dish.

PS:
It can be served
with mashed
potatoes, fried
potatoes,
tomatoes or with
green
peppers.

48

INGREDIENTS

750 g. minced lamb (minced twice)
1-5 glass of bulgur (boiled and pounded wheat)
3 eggs
3 onions
2 tblsp butter
1 glass of oil for frying
1 tbsp. currants
2 tbsps. pine nuts or pistachios
1 cup of shelled walnuts
black peper, salt, cummin, red pepper
1/2 bunch of parsley

STUFFED MEATBALLS
İÇLİ KÖFTE

COOKING

- Stuffing: Fry the chopped onions together with pine nuts or pistachios in 2 tblsps. of butter. Add half of the meat and stir well. Add crushed walnuts, salt, red pepper, cummin, chopped parsley and currants, stirring well.
- Mix half of the meat with bulgur, salt, black pepper, red pepper, 1 egg and 1/2 glass of water, for 30 minutes.
- Divide the mixture and shape into an oval in wet palms. Hollow out each ball until it is like an empty egg shell. Stuff the balls with the previously made stuffing mixture.
- Put 7-8 glasses of water into a saucepan, boil it with some salt. Boil the balls in the water for 15-20 minutes. Strain the balls and dip them in beaten eggs then fry them in hot oil.

PS:
Meatballs can be served with salad and ayran (yogurt drink)

PS:
Meatballs can be served with mashed patatoes, fried patatoes, tomatoes or pepper,

MEATBALLS IN EGG SAUCE (Serves 6)

TERBİYELİ KÖFTE

INGREDIENTS
750 g. minced lamb
1 cup of rice
1 medium sized onion
1/2 bunch of parsley
2 eggs
1 lemon
1 tbsp. butter
salt, black pepper, red pepper
3 tbsp. flour

COOKING
- Egg sauce: Beat 2 egg yolks together with lemon juice.
- Mix grated onion, washed rice, chopped parsley, salt, black pepper and minced meat. Knead for 5 minutes. Wetting the palms with water, break off small walnut-sized lumps of the mixture and form into balls.
- Place the balls into a floured tray. Shake the tray to coat the balls with flour.
- Boil in enough salted water to cover the meatballs.
- Add some boiling water from the meat ball's pan to the egg sauce and stir well. Pour the mixture over boiling meat balls. Boil for a further minute and remove from heat.
- (Before serving) Pour over the sauce made from the melted butter and red pepper.

AUBERGINE KEBAB (Serves 10)
PATLICAN KEBAP

INGREDIENTS
1 kg. long and large
   aubergines
4-5 tomatoes
10-15 green peppers
750 g. minced lamb
   (minced twice)
salt and black pepper

COOKING
- Mix minced meat, salt and black pepper. Shape the mixture into balls.
- Wash the aubergines and squeeze out the excess water and cut them into circular slices, 1 1/2 - 2 cm. wide.
- Place the circular slices of aubergines on the skewers alternating the meat balls and aubergines. Grill on barbecue.
- Remove the meat and aubergines from the skewers. Put in a big bowl or dish. Cut the tomatoes and green peppers into 4 pieces then cook them over the charcoal. Then place them over the aubergines and cover the dish. Cook it over a low heat 1-2 minutes. Let it stand for half an hour before serving.

PS: Aubergine kebab in oven:

Prepared aubergines and meatballs are placed in a shallow pan and put into oven.

Just before well cooked, take the pan out and arrange tomatoes together with peppers on top.

Put dots of butter on top of the pan then return to the oven. Cook until the tomatoes and peppers are lightly brown.

SHISH KEBAB (Serves 10)
ŞİŞ KEBAP

INGREDIENTS

1 kg. cubed lamb
   (for shish)
3 tomatoes
6 long green peppers
1/2 cup of olive oil
1 lemon
1 tsp. thyme
1 onion
salt and black pepper

COOKING

❦ Place the meat in a bowl, pour over the oil and lemon juice, add thyme,sliced onion, salt and black pepper, mix well and leave to marinate for 4-5 hours.

❦ Cut the green peppers and tomatoes the same size as the meat.

❦ Place the cubes of meat on the skewers alternately with the tomato, and pepper. Grill on barbecue above charcoal.

BRAISED LAMB WITH RICE (Serves 5)

PİLAVLI TAS KEBAB

INGREDIENTS
750 g. lamb
(cut into cubes)
4 medium sized
onions
5-6 long green
peppers
4 tomatoes
2 tbsps. butter
salt, black pepper,
thyme
1 glass of uncooked
rice.
1-5 glass of hot
water.

COOKING

❧ Melt the butter. Fry the onions cut into quarters, long green peppers, and brown cubed meat. Add peeled chopped tomatoes and continue to cook for 3 minutes more. Add salt, black pepper, thyme and 4-5 glasses of hot water and cook a further 10 minutes.

❧ Gather the meat and the vegetables in the middle of the saucepan and cover them with a bowl. Put the lid on and simmer for about an hour until the meat is tender.

❧ Put 1 glass of rice in a separate bowl and cover it with hot water. Let it wait for 20 minutes then strain through a sieve.

❧ Place the meat and vegetables in the middle of a separate saucepan, then again cover them with a bowl. Around the bowl, place the washed rice. Add 1.5 glasses of water or meat stock, and salt. Put the lid on and simmer until the rice is tender. Serve hot.

PULSES WITH MEAT
(Serves 10)
ETLİ KURU BAKLAGİLLER

INGREDIENTS
(Chick-peas, white beans,
barbunya; similar to
kidney but marbled,)

2 glasses of pulses

500 g. cubed meat

2 tbsps. butter

2 medium sized onions

3-4 long green peppers

2 tomatoes

1 tblsp. tomato paste

1 tsp. salt

black pepper.

COOKING

- ✻ Soak pulses overnight. Drain, add 3 glasses of water and boil until not quite tender.
- ✻ Chop onions and sauté in butter with minced beef in a saucepan. Stir well to prevent the mince forming lumps.
- ✻ Add tomato paste, peeled and chopped tomatoes, long green peppers and cooked pulses. Stir.
- ✻ Add 3 glasses of hot water. Cook over a moderate heat until the meat and the pulses are tender.
- ✻ Add salt to taste 10 minutes before serving. Serve hot.

FOREST KEBAB (Serves 10)
ORMAN KEBAP

INGREDIENTS
1 kg. lamb (shoulder /shank cut into cubes)
2 onions
3 potatoes
3 carrots
1 glass of peas (tinned)
1 tsp flour
3 tbsps. butter
salt, thyme

COOKING

- In a saucepan fry the meat and chopped onions in butter. Add the flour and stir for a further minute. Then add 4 glasses of hot water while stirring. Cook over a medium heat until the meat is tender.
- Add the potatoes cut into small pieces together with carrots cut into finger sized pieces. When the vegetables are tender, add tinned peas, salt and thyme. Cook for a further 5 minutes then serve.

BEEF WITH TOMATO PASTE (Serves 5)
SALÇALI BİFTEK

INGREDIENTS
1 kg. beef steak
4 tbsps. butter
2 onions
5 tomatoes or
2 tbsps. tomato paste
3 bay leaves
1 cup wine
salt, black pepper

COOKING
- Fry the steak on both sides over a low heat in half the butter. Place them in a tray.
- Chop the onions and then sauté in the remaning butter. Add chopped tomatoes or tomato paste.Stir well. Add wine, 2 glasses of water and boil on a low heat till cooked.
- Pour the tomato sauce over the steak. Add salt and place the bay leaves over it. Cook with the lid on until the steak is tender (in oven or over a low heat).

KEBAB WITH BECHEMAL SAUCE
(Serves 6) BEŞAMEL SALÇALI KEBAB

INGREDIENTS
1 kg.lamb (cut into cubes)
2 onions
3 tbsps. butter
1 tbsp. flour
1 glass of milk
salt, black pepper
2 eggs

COOKING
- Melt the butter in a deep pan. Sauté the meat together with chopped onions. (Let the meat juice evaporate)
- Add 2 glasses of hot water, salt and black pepper, cook until the meat is tender and the meat juice has evaporated.
- Place the meat in a serving dish.
- Fry the flour and butter in a seperate pan until golden brown. Add milk gradually. Cool, then add 2 eggs, salt and black pepper. Stir well.
- Pour the mixture over the meat in a serving dish. Put grated cheese on top and cook in the oven until golden brown. Serve hot.

LAMB CASSEROLE (Serves 5)
KUZU GÜVEÇ

COOKING

❦ Put 1 tbsp. butter into the casserole. Place in cubed meat. Cut onions and tomatoes in rings then place them over the meat. Dice the pepper and garlic and put them on top.

❦ Sprinkle on salt and black pepper. On top add bay leaves, the rest of the butter and then 1/2 cup of water. Cover it with aluminium foil and place it in a moderate oven.

❦ Bake for about 30 minutes. Serve hot.

INGREDIENTS
750 g. lamb (cut into cubes)
7-8 tomatoes
3 medium sized onions
10 long green peppers
7-8 cloves of garlic
1-2 bay leaves
2 tbsps. butter
salt, black pepper

ROAST LEG OF LAMB (Serves 10)
ROSTO

INGREDIENTS
1 leg of lamb (1,5 kg.)
2 tbsps. butter
1 tbsp. tomato paste
1 tbsp. flour
8 glasses of hot water
2 chopped onions
200 g. carrots
200 g.chopped clery
1/2 tsp. thyme
2 bay leaves
salt and black pepper.

COOKING
- Melt the butter in a saucepan. Dip the lamb in salt on both sides then fry until golden brown. Add the tomato paste and flour, and fry for a further 2 minutes. Pour hot water over it.
- Add and boil chopped onions, carrot, celery, bay - leaves, salt, black pepper and thyme. Cook over a moderate heat for 1,5 hours.
- When it is cooked, there should be approximetley 2,5 glasses of tomato sauce in the saucepan. If it is less than that, add some more hot water and cook it for a further 10 minutes.
- Place the cooked meat in a serving dish. Pour the strained tomato sauce over it. Slice and serve.

POACHED LAMB SHOULDER (Serves 5)
KUZU KAPAMA

INGREDIENTS

1 kg. lamb shoulder (In 5 pieces)
1 tbsp. butter.
15 spring onions
1 lettuce
1/2 bunch of chard
1 bunch of dill
salt, black pepper
2 glasses of hot water.

COOKING

- Place the meat in a saucepan. Pour over 2 glasses of water to just cover the meat and then boil. Just before it is compelety cooked take off the heat and wash the meat in cold water. Place it in a saucepan without water.
- Add salt, black pepper, and again 2 glasses of hot water to the meat. Add sliced spring onions, lettuce cut into small pieces and 1/2 bunch of chard, together with dill. Cook it over a low heat for an hour and 15 minutes. Serve.

KEBAB IN A PAPER BAG (Serves 6)

KAĞIT KEBABI

INGREDIENTS

6 sheets of greaseproof paper
  (30x35 cm.)
1 kg. lamb (not on the bone)
2 tbsps. butter
200 g. shallots.
1 glass of peas (tinned)
salt, black pepper
1 tsp. thyme
1/2 bunch of dill

COOKING

* Put the chopped meat in a deep pan. Add 1 tblsp melted butter, salt, black pepper and thyme then stir well.
* Melt the other half of the butter. Spread it over 6 pieces of greaseproof paper (30x35 cm). Place the meat in the middle of each piece of paper. On top, place the peeled shallots. Fold the edges of the paper over it like a package. Then arrange on a baking tray, folded sides downwards. Bake at 180°C with lid on, for about 1,5 hours.
* Before serving, open the paper a little and add peas and chopped dill, and serve.

COVERED BEEF (Serves 5)

KAPLANMIŞ BİFTEK

INGREDIENTS

10 cutlets
50 g. grated cheese
300 g. potatoes (boiled)
4 eggs
2 tbsps. flour
2 tbsps. butter
1 glass of oil (for frying)
salt, black pepper

COOKING

🐃 Salt the cutlets and sprinkle them with pepper. Melt the butter in a deep pan and fry them until golden brown on both sides.

🐃 Mix grated potatoes, grated cheese, flour, salt, black pepper and egg together. Add water to form a thick cream-like consistency.Stir well.

🐃 Coat the cutlets in the mixture and fry until golden brown on both sides.

🐃 Drain on a piece of kitchen paper and place them in a serving dish.

COLD MEAT WITH JELLY (Serves 6)
JÖLELİ SOĞUK ET

INGREDIENTS
2 calf tongues
5-6 cucumber pickles
2 hard - boiled eggs
2 carrots (boiled)
1 medium sized onion
1/2 bunch of parsley
stems
2-3 celery stalks
salt, black pepper
9 leaves of gelatine

COOKING

❧ Cut the thick surface of the tongues and wash. Boil the quartered onions, parsley stems, celery stalks, black pepper, salt and 5 glasses of cold water together with the tongues in a pressure-cooker for half an hour.

❧ When the tongues are cool, cut them into small pieces.

❧ Add the gelatine leaves to the remaining. Stir and melt.

❧ Put 1/4 of the gelatine mixture in a meat tin and set. When it is set, arrange sliced eggs, cucumber pickles and carrots over it. Put the pieces of meat over and around the jelly. Place Russian salad in the center and cover it with meat.

❧ Pour the remaining gelatine mixture over the meat, then again set it in the fridge. (not in the deep-freeze)

❧ Before serving let the tin wait in warm water for about 2-3 seconds - then turn upside down onto a serving dish.

FRIED LIVER (Serves 6)
CİĞER TAVA

INGREDIENTS
1 lamb's liver
2 tbsps. flour
1/2 bunch of parsley
20-25 spring onions
salt, black pepper, red pepper, sumach
1 glass of olive oil
Juice of 1/2 lemon

COOKING
- Remove the tissue and dice the liver into small cubes. Coat the pieces in flour and fry them while stirring. Add salt and black pepper.
- Mix salt, red pepper, sumach, chopped parsley, lemon juice, chopped onion and 2 tbsps. of oil in a separate bowl.
- Place the fried liver in the center of a serving dish and garnish it with the onion mixture. It is ready to serve.

CIRCASSIAN CHICKEN (Serves 10)
ÇERKEZ TAVUĞU

INGREDIENTS
1 chicken
3-4 glasses of shelled walnuts
3 slices of stale bread
3 tsps. black pepper
3-4 bunches of parsley
3 tblsps. olive oil
salt

COOKING

- Boil the chicken until tender. When the chicken is cool remove the meat from the bones and cut into bite-sized pieces. Place the pieces in a serving dish and sprinkle with salt and black pepper.
- In a blender chop the walnuts. Add half of the stale bread and half of the red pepper. Chop again. Add the rest of the stale bread and red pepper and 2 tbsps of olive oil.
- Put the chopped walnut mixture in a serving dish. Gradually add the chicken stock to the walnut mixture. If the walnut mixture turns lumpy, strain it. Stir the mixture over the chicken pieces.
- Garnish with the remaining oil and parsley.

FISH WITH MAYONNAISE (Serves 5)
MAYONEZLİ BALIK

INGREDIENTS

1 kg. Sea - Bass
(Lesser gray mullet or Bonito)
1 medium sized onion
salt, black pepper
2 bay - leaves

For the Russion Salad:
2 egg - yolks
1/5 glasses of olive oil
1/2 lemon
1 tsp. mustard powder

2 potatoes (boiled)
2 carrots (boiled)
1/2 glass of peas (tinned)
12 small cucumber pickles.

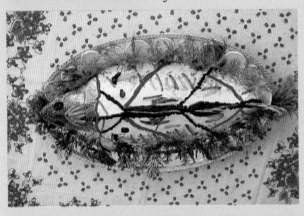

COOKING

❦ Gut and clean the fish, then cut into 2-3 pieces. Place the pieces into boiling water. Add a quartered onion, salt, black pepper and bay leaves. Boil the mixture. Let it cool in the stock. Cut the pieces of fish into small pieces and add salt and black pepper.

❦ Put egg-yolks, salt and mustard into a china bowl. Mix it while adding the olive oil drop by drop. Add the lemon juice in the same way. Add carrots cut into small cubes, potatoes, pickles and peas, salt and mustard. Stir well. (Leave aside 3 tblsps. of the mixture before adding the vegetables)

❦ Mix the fish pieces and russian salad. Place in a serving dish. Put the left over mayonnaise on top and garnish it with parsley, pickles and hard boiled eggs.

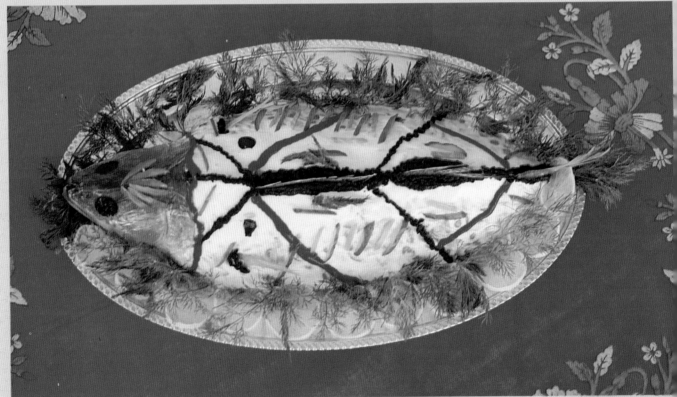

SEA-BASS IN PAPER BAGS (Serves 5)

YAĞLI KAĞITTA LEVREK

INGREDIENTS

5 Sea-Bass fillets (15 g. each)
sheets of greaseproof paper (50x70 cm.)
1 tbsp. butter
3 medium sized tomatoes
1 tbsp. onion (chopped)
1-2 bay leaves
1/2 cup of white wine
1 cup of water
1/2 bunch of chopped parsley
salt

COOKING

- Fold the greaseproof paper and cut it into heart like shapes. Spread the butter on one side of the pieces.
- Melt the butter in a saucepan. Fry the fillets and chopped onions until golden brown. Then add chopped mushrooms, white wine, bay leaves, salt and water. Cook for 10 minutes with lid on. (Over a low heat) Let the fish almost absorb the stock.
- Put the fish into another dish. Add chopped parsley to the remaing sauce.
- Put fish onto the greaseproof paper. Pour over some fish sauce, fold the edges to cover the fish (fold each side downwards).
- Place the packets onto an oven tray and bake in a hot oven for a further 5 minutes. Serve in the

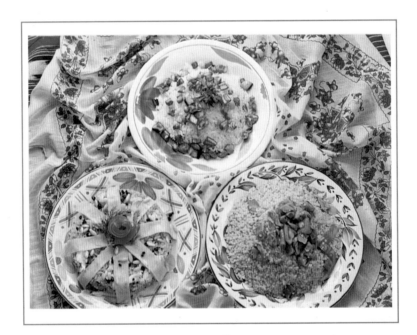

Rice and Savouries

ORIENTAL PILAFF (Serves 6)
(RICE FOR STUFFING) İÇ PİLAV

INGREDIENTS
2 glasses of rice
3-5 glasses of meat stock
2-5 tbsps. butter
1/2 lamb liver
50 gm. pine nuts
50 gm. currants
salt, black pepper
1 glass of walnuts
1/2 bunch of dill

COOKING
- Pick over the rice and wash. Place in a bowl and cover it with hot water. Stir in 2 tbsps. of salt and leave to soak until the water cools. Strain and wash well.
- Place the butter in a pan, add nuts and sauté until brown. Place the strained rice into the pan. Turn the heat up and stir for 10 minutes. Add salt, black pepper, washed currants and 3-5 glasses of hot stock.
- With the pan lid on, cook first over a high heat then over a low heat until the rice absorbs the liquid.
- Melt a tbsp. of butter in a pan. Sauté the boiled and cubed liver in it. Add a glass of crushed walnuts and cook for a further 2 minutes. Warm the cooked liver and arrange it over the rice.

RICE WITH CUBED LAMB
(Serves 6)
ETLİ PİLAV

INGREDIENTS
250 g. lamb (cut in cubes)
2 glasses of rice
3 tomatoes or
1,5 tbsps. tomato paste
2-5 tbsps. butter
1 medium sized onion
salt, black pepper
3,5 glasses of water

COOKING

❦ Pick over and wash the rice then place it in a bowl and cover with hot water. Add 2 tbsps. salt and leave it to soak until the rice is tender. (30 minutes)

❦ Melt the butter in a deep pan. Add the cubed meat and chopped onions, stir occasionally until the juice of the meat is released. Add washed and chopped tomatoes or tomato paste and stir well.

❦ Add salt, black pepper and 5 glasses of hot water. Cook it all together until the meat is tender.

❦ When the meat is tender, there should be $3^{1/2}$ glasses of liquid.

❦ Add the sieved rice.

❦ With the pan lid on, cook it first over a high heat and then over a low heat until the rice absorbs the liquid.

❦ Finally remove the pan from the heat and let the rice rest for about 20 minutes before serving.

RICE IN PHYLLO SHEETS
YUFKALI PİLAV

INGREDIENTS

2 glasses of chicken stock
3/5 cup of pistachios
1/2 cup of currants
1/2 cup of shelled almonds
1 small chicken
3 tbsps. butter
salt, black pepper

DOUGH

1-5 glasses of flour
2 eggs
100 g. butter
1/2 cup of pistachios (shelled)
salt

COOKING

❦ Boil the chicken. Strain and separate the meat from the bones. Cut the chicken meat into bite-sized pieces.

❦ Melt 3 tbsps. of butter in a saucepan. Sauté the pistachios and almonds until golden brown. Strain and put them aside.

❦ Pick over the rice and place it in a bowl; cover with hot water. Add 2 tbsps. salt and leave it to soak until the water cools. After straining, add the rice to the melted butter. Stir for a further 2 minutes and add hot chicken stock. Cook first over a high heat and then over a medium heat until the water is absorbed by the rice. Let the rice rest for 15 minutes.

❦ Add the sautéed pistachios, almonds, washed currants and chicken pieces, salt and black pepper into the cooked rice. Stir all together well without breaking up the rice grains.

❦ Sift the flour into a pan, make a hollow in the center and break in the eggs; add butter, salt and a little water, knead well. After making a hard dough, flatten it slightly for about 2-3 mm. thick and cut into lengthways 1 cm wide each.

❦ Take a circular and well greased oven tray and line it. Put the phyllo sheets lengthwise and widthwise into the tin but leave a space between them. (like a cage). Place shelled pistachios into these spaces. Add rice on top and press over by hand. Fold the drape over sides of the sheets on top of the rice. Finally cook in a moderate oven until both sides are golden brown.

❦ Turn up side down before serving.

RICE WITH AUBERGINES (Serves 6)
PATLICANLI PİLAV

COOKING

INGREDIENTS

2 glasses of rice

3 tbsps. butter

3,5 glasses of meat stock

2 aubergines (seedless)

1 glass of oil (for frying)

salt

❧ Pick over the rice and wash. Then place it in a bowl and cover it with hot water. Stir in a tbsp. of salt and leave to soak until the water cools.

❧ Melt the butter in a saucepan. Add the strained rice and sauté rapidly for 1 or 2 minutes. Pour over the meat stock, bring to the boil then reduce the heat and cook until the liquid is absorbed. Cook with pan lid on.

❧ Wash and drain aubergines. Peel lenghthwise and cut into 4 pieces then cut into cubes. Fry in hot oil and when golden brown, remove from pan. Drain off excess oil using a sieve.

❧ Place the fried aubergines over the rice. Stir well and let the rice rest before serving.

CRACKED WHEAT WITH MEAT (Serves 6)
ETLİ BULGUR PİLAVI

INGREDIENTS :

2 glasses of cracked wheat

4 glasses of meat stock

3 medium sized onions

3 tomatoes or

2 tbsps. tomato paste

4 tbsps. butter

250 g. cubed lamb

salt, black pepper.

COOKING

- ❧ Melt the butter in a saucepan. Sauté the chopped onions and cubed meat together.
- ❧ Peel the tomatoes, take the seeds out and cut into cubes (or add tomato paste). Add these cubes to the mixture and stir well.
- ❧ Add 5-6 glasses of meat stock, salt, black pepper and cook until the meat is tender.
- ❧ When the meat is tender, (there should be about 4 glasses of liquid left) add the cracked weat and stir well. Cook over a medium heat until the water is absorbed and the cracked wheat is tender.
- ❧ Let it rest before serving.

CRACKED WHEAT WITH LENTILS (Serves 6)
MERCİMEKLİ BULGUR PİLAVI

INGREDIENTS :

2 glasses of pounded weat

4 glasses of meat stock

2 onions

4 tblsps. butter

1 cup of green lentils

3 tomatoes or

2 tbsps. tomato paste

salt, black and red pepper.

COOKING

❧ Pick over the lentils. Put them in a bowl and cover with warm water overnight. Boil till tender. Drain and wash 2 or 3 times.

❧ Melt the butter in a pan, add the chopped oninons and brown. Add peeled and chopped tomatoes or tomato paste, 4 glasses of hot stock, salt, black and red pepper. Stir well and bring to boil.

❧ When boiling, add sieved lentils together with cracked wheat and cook over a medium heat until the wateris absorbed.

❧ Let stand for 10-15 minutes before serving.

A RAVIOLI-LIKE DISH WITH YOGURT
(Serves 10)
MANTI
INGREDIENTS
2 glasses of flour
1 egg
250 g. minced meat
1 onion
1/2 bunch of parsley
salt and black pepper
500 g. yogurt
4-5 cloves of garlic
3-4 tbsps. butter

COOKING
- Sift the flour into a mixing bowl, make a hollow in the center and into this break the egg, add salt and 1-2 tbsps. of water. Knead well. Put the dough aside in a warm place for 5 minutes under a damp cloth.
- Cut the dough into 2-3 pieces. Place each piece of dough onto a floured surface and coat with flour on both sides. Roll out to approxomately 1-2 mm. sized thickness. Cut the dough into 6 cm. squares.
- Mix the minced meat and grated onion, season with salt and pepper to taste. Add chopped parsley and knead well.
- Place a hazel nut-sized minced meat filling in the center of each square of the dough and picking up the corners of each square pinch them together into a little bundle shape or fold each square into a triangle shape.
- Place the bundles on a greased baking tray. Brush each bundle with butter and bake in a medium oven until brown.
- Place browned bundles into a saucepan. Pour over 5-6 glasses of hot water or meat stock. Add salt and cook until the bundles are soft.
- After serving, pour over some yogurt with crushed garlic in it. Finally pour the melted butter. Sprinkle paprika over the top before serving.

WATER PASTRY PIE

SU BÖREĞİ

(Serves 10)

INGREDIENTS
500 g. flour
10 eggs
250 g. butter
1 bunch of parsley
1 bunch of dill
250 g. cheese
1 glass of milk
salt

COOKING

- ❦ Sift the flour. Make a hollow in the center and into this break 10 eggs. Add salt and a little hot water. Knead well and divide the dough into 12 equal pieces. Put them aside under a damp cloth for 20 minutes.

- ❦ Take each piece of the pastry and roll it out each piece with a long thin Turkish rolling pin. Dusting the rolling pin with flour, roll out each piece about 2-3 mm.thick. First boil each rolled out sheet of pastry in salty water then remove the sheets very carefully out of the boiling hot water and place them in another pan filled with cold water. As the last step remove them from the cold water and dry them with a cloth.

- ❦ Place one of these sheets into a greased oven tray. Sprinkle the pastry in the tray lightly with melted butter. In the same way place the remaining 6 sheets of pastry into the tray pouring melted butter between each sheet. Over the 6th sheet spread the filling: cheese, milk, parsley, dill and I egg. Over this spread the remaining sheets of pastry speading each with melted butter. Spread the remaing butter on top and cook until golden brown.

PS :
The filling can be put
in the centre,
or spread between
each layer of pastry.

PUFF PASTRY MEAT SAVOURY (Serves 5)
TALAŞ BÖREĞİ

INGREDIENTS

Ingredients for the phyllo sheets:
300 g. flour
250 g. butter
1/2 lemon
1 cup of warm water
2-3 tsps. salt

Filling:
1/2 kg. lamb (cut in cubes)
1 medium sized onion
1 tblsp. butter
1 tblsp. tomato paste
salt, black and red pepper.

COOKING

- Sift the flour into a mixing bowl making a hollow in the center. Add salt, lemon juice and a cup of warm water, then knead it into a soft dough. Set aside under a damp cloth for 15 minutes.
- Roll out the pastry dusting both sides with flour leaving the middle thicker. Place the butter in the center of the pastry, fold the edges like a small package. Flour and roll out the pastry lengthways in a rectangular shape. Fold both ends into the center, then fold in half. Set aside under a damp cloth for 30 minutes.
- Flour the pastry and roll out lengthways again in a rectangular shape. Fold it in a book shape then set aside for a further 30 minutes. Repeat the same procedure three times more.
- Then roll it out to 3 mm. thickness and cut into squares each 10 cm. Place the filling in the center of each 10 cm. square. Fold the corners over the filling into the center to form a packet and arrange them on a baking tray (the folded parts downwards). Brush with beaten egg yolk and bake in a hot oven until golden brown.

FILLING

Brown the meat and chopped onion together with butter. Add tomato paste and stir well. Add 2 glasses of hot water and cook until the meat is tender. Strain the gravy and sprinkle salt, black and red pepper over the meat. Leave to cool.

ALTERNATIVE FILLINGS FOR PASTRIES ARE BELOW
DEĞİŞİK BÖREKLER

After arranging sheets of water pastry in a baking tray, you may use different stuffings mentioned below.

CHEESE FILLING

250 g. white cheese.

1/2 bunch of parsley

1/2 bunch of dill

1 egg white

black and red pepper

MİNCED LAMB FILLING

250 g. minced lamb
1 medium sized onion
1/2 bunch of parsley
1 tbsp. butter
salt and black pepper.

POTATO FILLING

2 boiled potatoes
200 g. minced lamb
1 medium sized onion
1 tbsp. butter
1/2 bunch of parsley
salt, black and
red pepper.

COOKING
❧ Wash the cheese and mash it with a fork.
❧ Add egg white, chopped parsley and dill, red and black pepper. Mix well.

COOKING
❧ Brown the meat and finely chopped onion together with butter in a saucepan.
❧ Add chopped potatoes and parsley, red and black pepper. Stir well.

COOKING
❧ Brown the meat and finely chopped onion together with butter in a saucepan.
❧ Add chopped parsley. salt and black pepper. Stir well.

INGREDIENTS

500 g. flour
2 tbsps. butter
2 glasses of oil (for frying)
1 egg
2 tsps. salt
1/4 bunch of parsley
1/4 bunch of dill
250 g. cheese
1 cup of warm water
black pepper.

SAVOURY PUFF PASTRY PIE
PUF BÖREĞİ

COOKING

- Sift the flour in a mixing bowl. Make a hollow in the center and into it break 1 egg; add 1 tbsp. butter, 1 tsp. salt, 1 cup of warm water. Knead well into a soft dough.
- Roll out the dough very thinly into a circle 4 cm in diameter. Cut it into 6-7 equal pieces.
- By using a long thin rolling pin, roll out each piece dusting both sides with flour until about 2 mm. thick.
- Melt and cool the rest of the butter.
- Brush one side of the sheet with butter. Place the sheets on top of each other and cover them with a damp cloth. Set aside for half an hour. Roll out again until 1-2 mm. thick dusting with flour to prevent sticking.
- Place a spoon of the cheese, parsley, dill and black pepper mixture on top of each circle. Fold in half thus making a semi-circle and press the edges firmly.

- Fry each pie in frying oil shaking lightly until golden brown.
- Before serving, drain on a piece of kitchen paper.

INGREDIENTS
3 Phyllo sheets
1 glass of oil (for frying)
250 g. cheese
1/2 bunch of
parsley
black and red
pepper.

CIGARETTE SHAPED SAVOURIES
SİGARA BÖREĞİ

COOKING
* Placing the phyllo sheets on top of each other, cut them into 4,then cut each 1/4 sheet into half so that you will have 8 triangles from each sheet.
* Mix cheese, parsley, black pepper and red pepper for the filling.
* Place the filling across the base of each triangle, leaving a centimeter at the sides. Roll them up into a cigar shape by folding the sides into the centre . Damp the end of the pastry to stick it down.
* Fry in hot oil shaking firmly until golden brown.
* Before serving drain on a piece of paper towel.

Desserts

ASHURA (Serves 12)

AŞURE

INGREDIENTS

3 glasses of whole wheat
1/2 glass of rice
1/2 glass white beans
1/2 glass chickpeas
1/2 glass raisons (seedless)
10 dried figs
10 dried apricots
4-5 slices of orange rind
1/2 cup rose water
1 packet of vanilla
1 glass of shelled walnuts or hazelnuts
3 tbsps. grated coconut.
3 tsps. cinnamon
6 glasses of sugar

COOKING

❦ Pick over and soak the whole wheat, chickpeas and beans separately in water overnight.

❦ Boil the wheat, rice and chopped orange rind in fresh water until they are soft and mushy. (over a medium heat for 4-5 hours).

❦ Place the wheat, rice and orange rind into a separate pan. Add boiled chickpeas and beans to this and boil altogether.

❦ Add sugar, currants, diced figs and apricots, vanilla and rose water. Cook them for a further 10-15 minutes.

❦ Pour into individual bowls and when cool, garnish each bowl with crushed nuts, cinnamon and grated coconut.

87

PUMPKIN DESSERT
(Serves 6) KABAK TATLISI

INGREDIENTS

1 kg Pumpkın
3 glasses of sugar
1 glass of coarsly chopped walnuts
1 tbsp. grated coconut.

COOKING

❦ Cut the pumpkin into large wedges. Clean away the seeds and green parts, wash and slice it into 2 cm. thick and 5-7 cm long pieces.

❦ In a pan arrange a layer of pumpkin slices with sugar on top. Put another a layer of pumpkin slices and sugar on top. Put the lid on and set aside overnight. Pour over half a cup of water and cook over a medium heat until the pumkin slices are tender and the water is absorbed.

❦ When cool, transfer the pumpkin pieces into a serving dish and sprinkle ground walnuts and grated coconut on top.

SEMOLINA HELVA-İRMİK HELVASI -(Serves 8)

INGREDIENTS
250 g. coarse
   semolina
125 g. butter
500 g. sugar
1.5 tbsps. pine nuts
1/2 lt. milk.

COOKING

❧ Melt the butter in a saucepan, add semolina and pine nuts. Brown until golden.

❧ Add sugar and milk; stir well.

❧ Put a lid on the saucepan and cook until the water is absorbed.

❧ Let stand for 15 minutes then sprinkle over a cup of sugar. Put the lid on again and set aside to cool before serving.

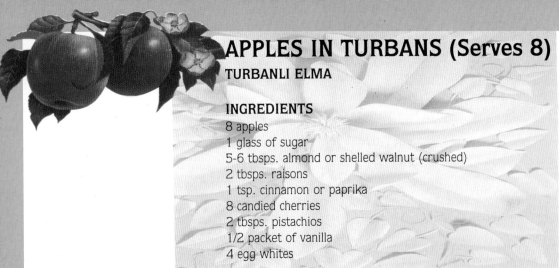

APPLES IN TURBANS (Serves 8)

TURBANLI ELMA

INGREDIENTS

8 apples
1 glass of sugar
5-6 tbsps. almond or shelled walnut (crushed)
2 tbsps. raisons
1 tsp. cinnamon or paprika
8 candied cherries
2 tbsps. pistachios
1/2 packet of vanilla
4 egg whites

COOKING

❧ Hollow out the centers of the apples, peel and wash them.

❧ Cook the apples in 1 glass of water together with 1 glass of sugar.

❧ When the apples are tender, take them out of the saucepan with a fork. Arrange them in an oven proof dish leaving a 3 cm space between each one.

❧ Mix crushed almonds or walnuts, raisons, cinnamon, vanilla and 1 tblsp. sugar together, then stuff the mixture into the hole in each apple.

❧ Beat the egg whites in a bowl till fluffy. Add the syrup left from the apples and stir well. When the cream is prepared, spread it over apples, start doing this from the middle to the top. It should have the shape of a turban.

❧ Garnish the top with a candied cherry, orange rinds, or crushed pistachios.

INGREDIENTS

250 g. sugar
100 g. uncooked rice
1 lt. milk
1/4 fresh grated coconut
3 tbsps. pistachio
6 tbsps. blanched almonds

ALMOND CREAM (Serves 5)
KEŞKÜL

COOKING

- Pick over and wash the rice. Soak in a bowl of water overnight. The next day crush the rice in a bowl.
- Crush the grated coconut and half of the almonds in a bowl.
- Boil the milk in a copper tin.
- Put the crushed rice, coconut, nuts and almonds into the milk.
- Cook it over a low heat while stirring.
- Pour the mixture into separate bowls and sprinkle the top of each with pistachios, grated coconut and almonds.

BAKED RICE PUDDING
(Serves 6) FIRINDA SÜTLAÇ

INGREDIENTS
1 lt. milk
1/2 glass of uncooked rice
1 glass of sugar
2 egg-yolks
1 tbsp. starch
1/2 packet of vanilla

COOKING
- ❦ Bring 1 glass of water to the boil. Add rice and cook until the rice has absorbed all the water.
- ❦ Add milk and sugar, cook for a further 15 minutes.
- ❦ Beat the egg yolks. Mix the starch in 1/2 cup of water. Then mix it into the beaten yolks. Take 5-6 tbsps. of pudding mixture from the rice pudding and add it to the egg mixture. After stirring well, pour it into the boiling pudding. Stir well.
- ❦ Take off the heat and add vanilla.
- ❦ Place in individual ovenproof bowls and arrange the bowls in an oven tray with a little water in it. Brown the tops, and serve cold.

INGREDIENT
1/2 lt. milk
3 eggs
1-5 glasses of flour
1 tsp. salt
grated rind of 1 lemon
1 glass of marmalade or jam
4-5 tbsps. melted butter.

CRÉPE SUZETTE (Serves 3)
KREP SUZET

COOKING
- Mix the eggs, flour, salt, grated lemon rinds. 1 tbsp. butter in a bowl. Add milk gradually, mix and stir well.
- Pour a ladle of this mixture into a greased pan (20 cm. diameter). Cook it on both sides by shaking the pan.
- Spread marmalade or jam on suzette and fold in half. Sprinkle on icing sugar before serving.

MILK AND CHICKEN BREAST-DESSERT (Serves 6)

TAVUK GÖĞSÜ

COOKING

- ❧ Wash the rice and leave it in hot water for an hour. Sieve and drain it well then crush in a bowl until it is like flour.
- ❧ Stir the flour into the milk. Add sugar, stir well and cook until the mixture thickens.
- ❧ Cut the well boiled breast into 2 cm. pieces and taking each piece between the thumb and the index finger of both hands, pick them into fine ligaments.
  Take two ladlesfull of the milk mixture and pour over the chicken ligaments. Mix and mash well with a fork.
- ❧ Put the mashed ligaments back into the pan and boil again. Stirring constantly, simmer this until the mixture has thickened sufficiently
- ❧ Pour in a ladlefull of chicken stock and remove from the heat.
- ❧ Pour the mixture into individual bowls which have been wetted with water. When they are cool turn them up side down into a serving dish. Sprinkle the top with cinnamon.

INGREDIENTS

1 lt milk

250 g. sugar

150 g. rice

1 cup of chicken stock

cinnamon

breast meat from half a chicken

INGREDIENTS

500 g. tel kadayıf
1.5 glasses of milk
200 g butter
25 g. shelled walnuts
4 glasses of sugar
2 glasses of water.
1/2 lemon

SWEET DESSERT (Serves 6)
TEL KADAYIF

COOKING

Syrup: Boil sugar and water then add one or two drops of lemon. Then put the half lemon into the liquid. Boil until the syrup thickens.

❧ Melt the butter and sprinkle half of it on the kadayıf. Place half of the butter and kadayıf into an oven proof dish (30-35 cm2 diameter). Sprinkle walnuts on top.

❧ Place the other half of the kadayıf over the walnuts and lightly press down. Pour over the rest of the melted butter.

❧ Bake in a medium oven until golden brown.

❧ Remove from the oven, pour over 1.5 glasses of hot milk, cover and set aside until soft.

❧ Pour over the warm syrup.

❧ When cold, cut into squares and place into serving dishes.

❧ If wanted, decorate with cream.

SEMOLINA DESSERT (Serves 8)
REVANİ

INGREDIENTS
6 eggs
250 g. butter
800 g. semolina
750 g. sugar
1/2 lemon
1 tbsp. icing sugar

Dessert:
- ❦ Put the butter, semolina and icing sugar in a bowl. Beat well with a wooden spoon until white. Beat the egg yolks into the mixture.
- ❦ In another bowl whip the 6 egg whites with a little salt until stiff (about 10 minutes). Add it quickly to the mixture mentioned above.
- ❦ Take a well greased cake tin and pour the mixture into it. Bake it in a moderate oven for 40 minutes.
- ❦ Put the cake into a bigger tin and pour over 3/4 of the syrup. Over a low heat let it absorb the syrup.
- ❦ Thicken the left over (1/4) syrup over a low heat and pour it over the semolina dessert.
- ❦ When cool, serve cut into slices.

COOKING

Syrup: Put sugar in a saucepan with water (this should completely cover the sugar). Heat. When it boils, add 1 tbsp. of lemon juice. While stirring well add half a lemon. Boil it until the syrup thickens.

INGREDIENTS :

250 g. flour
50 g. semolina
50 g. starch
100 g. butter
5 eggs
750 g. sugar
1/2 tbsp. lemon juice
salt
5 glasses of oil (for frying)

FLUTED - PASTRIES IN SYRUP
(Serves 6) TULUMBA TATLISI

Syrup: Cover the sugar with water and boil. Add lemon juice. Stir well until the syrup thickens.

COOKING:

- In another saucepan put 1,5 glasses of water, butter, a pinch of salt, 1 tbsp. sugar, then boil together. When boiling, add sifted flour, semolina and starch, stir quickly over a low heat (10 minutes)
- When the mixture is cool, break in the eggs and add a tbsp. of the syrup. Mix well.
- Put the dough into a pastry bag, squeeze out into long pieces with the help of a knife.
- Fry oil over a medium heat. Stir until they thicken and become golden brown.
- Drain well before tossing them into the pan of cool syrup.
- When they absorb the syrup, place them into a serving dish and garnish with pistachios.

ALMOND - PASTRIES IN SYRUP (Serves 6)

ŞEKERPARE

INGREDIENTS

250 g. flour
1 small packet of butter (125 g.)
75 g. icing sugar
2 egg-yolks
grated rind of 1 lemon
1/2 packet of vanilla
1 tbsp. lemon juice
1 tsp. baking powder
300 g. sugar
10-15 almonds

COOKING

Syrup: Place sugar and cover it compeletly with water, then bring it to the boil. Add 1/4 lemon juice. Boil together until the mixture thickens slightly.

- In another mixing bowl beat butter and 75 g. icing sugar until white.
- Mix well adding egg-yolks, vanilla, grated lemon rind, sifted flour and baking powder.
- Take large walnut size pieces of the dough and shape them first into balls then flatten slightly. Place them in a lightly greased baking tray at 1 cm. intervals, then press each piece of dough down in the center with your finger and press a blanched almond into each hollow.
- Bake in a moderate oven until golden brown.
- As soon as removed from the oven, pour on the syrup mentioned above. Let them absorb the syrup over a low heat.

DOUGHNUTS IN SYRUP (Serves 6)
"LADY'S NAVEL" - HANIM GÖBEĞİ

INGREDIENTS

250 g. flour
100 g. butter
4 eggs
1/2 tbsp. lemon juice
4-5 glasses of sugar
1 pinch of salt (1/2 tsp.)
4-5 glasses of oil
 (for frying)

COOKING

Syrup: Boil 4-5 glasses of water and 4,5 glasses of sugar in a saucepan. Add 1/2 tbsp. of lemon juice. Boil until the syrup thickens.

❧ In another saucepan boil 2 glasses of water, butter, and salt together. Toss in the sifted flour and stir vigorously with a wooden spoon.

❧ Remove from the heat, let it cool down slightly, break in the eggs one by one and knead well. Divide the dough into walnut sized pieces, shaping each into a flattened ball and then pierce the center with your finger.

❧ Pour the oil into a pan. Fry each flattened ball in the oil until golden brown.

❧ Toss the fried doughnuts into the syrup. And leave them to absorb the syrup for 5 minutes before placing them into a serving dish. If desired, garnish them with cream.

PS: Each time toss the flattened balls into cold oil.

"LOKMA" DOUGHNUTS (Serves 6)
LOKMA TATLISI

INGREDIENTS

For the Dough:
250 g. flour
1 tbsp. icing sugar
1 glass of oil
1 tbsp. yeast
1 egg
1 tsp. salt

Syrup:
1 kg. sugar
2 glasses of water
1/2 lemon juice
1 kg. oil
(for frying)

COOKING

- Mix all the ingredients for the dough in a bowl.
- The prepared dough is placed in a large bowl and then covered with a piece of cloth and set aside in a warm place to rise for 45 minutes.
- Boil the syrup ingredients mentioned above. Stir well and set aside to cool.
- Heat the oil.
- Squeeze the dough through your left fist. With a lightly oiled tea spoon, quickly cut and shape the dough into balls (walnut-sized) and drop them into the hot oil. Fry the balls until golden brown.
- Toss the fried balls into the cold syrup. After they absorb it, place them into a serving dish.

INGREDIENTS
4-5 glasses of flour
250 g. butter
2 eggs.
2 tbsps. of lemon juice
grated rind of 1 lemon
2 glasses of crushed
walnuts
4 glasses of sugar
1/2 tsp. salt.

BAKLAVA (Serves 10)

COOKING
Syrup: Boil 4 glasses of water, 4 glasses of sugar and 1/2 tbsp. lemon juice together until the syrup thickens.

- Sift 4 glasses of plain flour. Knead well with 1 egg, 1 tbsp. olive oil, salt, 1 tbsp. lemon juice, and 3/4 glass of water to produce a soft dough. Set aside under a wet cloth for 15-20 minutes.
- Roll out the dough 30 cm in diameter. Place the butter in the center and fold it like a packet. Dust it with flour and roll out lengthwise. Fold it like a packet and set aside under a wet cloth for 20 minutes.
- Roll out the dough lengthwise again and fold it like a packet, set aside under a wet piece of cloth for 20 minutes again (repeat the same procedure 3 times more).
- Roll out the dough until 4 mm. thick and cut it into squares (4-5 cm^2 each). Spread the finaly chopped walnut and sugar mixture in the middle and fold like a triangle. Place in a tray and brush with egg yolk. Bake in a moderate oven until golden brown.
- As soon as you remove baklava from the oven pour cold syrup on top. When it cools, it is ready to serve.

Cakes and Snacks

PLAIN CAKE (Serves 10)
SADE KEK

INGREDIENTS
6 eggs
2 glasses of flour
1,5 glasses of sugar
grated rind of 1/2 lemon
1 packet of vanilla

COOKING
❦ Beat the eggs and sugar with a mixer.
❦ Add sifted flour, vanilla and grated rind of 1/2 lemon.
Mix well.
❦ Pour the mixture into a greased and floured cake tin.
❦ Place into a warm oven and bake it at a
moderate heat.

INGREDIENTS:

3 eggs
1 glass of oil or 125 g. butter.
2,5 glasses of sugar
3,5 glasses of flour
3 glasses of grated carrot
grated rind of 1 lemon
1 glass of chopped walnut
1 tbsp. cinnamon
1 packet of vanilla
1/2 tbsp. baking powder.

COOKING

- Beat the eggs and sugar in a bowl.
- Add butter (or oil), grated carrots, lemon rind, walnuts, cinnamon, vanilla and baking powder. Mix well.
- Add sifted flour, continue to mix.
- Pour the mixture into a greased and floured cake tin. Bake in a moderate oven.

CARROT CAKE (Serves 10)
HAVUÇLU KEK

TEA CAKE (Serves 10)
ÇAYLI KEK

INGREDIENTS
3 glasses of flour
3 eggs
1,5 glasses of sugar
125 g. butter (melted)
1 glass of brewed tea
1 packet of baking powder
2 tbsps. cocoa
1/2 tbsp. cinnamon
1 glass of chopped walnuts.

COOKING
- Mix eggs, sugar, butter, brewed tea, cocoa, cinnamon and baking powder in a bowl.
- Add sifted flour to the mixture and continue to mix.
- Add walnuts.
- Pour into a greased and floured cake tin.
- Place the cake into a warm oven and bake it at moderate heat.

CAKE IN A TRAY
TEPSİ KEKİ
(SERVES 10)

INGREDIENTS

2 eggs
3 glasses of flour
125 g. butter
1/2 cups of olive oil
1 glass of yogurt
1 glass of sugar
1 packet of baking powder
   grated rind of 1/2 lemon
   juice of 1/2 lemon
1 glass of chopped
   walnuts.

COOKING:

- Beat the eggs and sugar in a bowl.
- Add melted butter, olive-oil, yogurt and grated lemon rind. Continue to mix.
- Add baking powder and lemon juice to the mixture and mix well.
- Add flour to form soft dough.
- Pour into a greased cake tin. Level the top and sprinkle chopped walnuts on top.
- Bake in 170°C oven until golden brown.

FIG CAKE (Serves 10)
İNCİRLİ KEK

INGREDIENTS :

3 eggs
1 glass of sugar
1,5 glass of flour
125 g. butter
1 packet of cinnamon
1 packet of baking powder
juice of 1/2 lemon
8 dried figs
1 cup of raisons
1 cup of walnuts

COOKING

❧ Chop walnuts and figs into small pieces and cover with a little water in a bowl for 15 minutes.

❧ Beat eggs and sugar; add butter, cinnamon, baking powder and lemon juice. Mix well.

❧ Add sifted flour and continue to stir. Add the chopped walnuts, figs, and raisons then put them into the dough. Mix together.

❧ Pour the mixture into a greased and floured baking tray. Bake in a moderate oven.

WALNUT COOKIES (Serves 10)
CEVİZLİ KURABİYE

INGREDIENTS
250 g. butter.
4 eggs
1 cup of yogurt
2 glasses of sugar
   grated rind of 1 lemon
1/2 tbsp. baking powder
1 tbsp. lemon juice.
   flour
1 glass of crushed walnuts

COOKING
❦ Mix butter, egg-yolks, yogurt, sugar,and grated lemon rind.
❦ Add baking powder and lemon juice, mix well.
❦ Add flour to form a soft dough.
❦ Shape into cookies. Brush each with egg white and sprinkle with chopped walnuts. Arrange them on a baking tray.
❦ Bake in a moderate oven until golden brown.

"FLOUR" COOKIES (Serves 10)
UN KURABİYESİ

INGREDIENTS
250 g. butter
250 g. icing sugar
4 glasses of flour
1 packet of vanilla

COOKING

- Mix butter, icing sugar and vanilla for 3-4 minutes in a bowl.
- Add flour and mix well to form a hard dough.
- Take walnut sized pieces of the dough and shape into rounds.
- Place on a baking tray. Bake in a moderate oven. The cookies should remain white.

The heat must come from the bottom of the oven.

INGREDIENTS

5 eggs
2 glasses of sugar
250 g. butter (melted)
1 glass of yogurt (mixed with a little water)
5 glasses of flour
1 packet of baking powder
juice 1/2 lemon
1 cup of raisons
1 cup of chopped walnuts
1 packet of vanilla
grated rind of 1/2 lemon.

COOKING

- Beat eggs and sugar for 5 minutes in a mixing bowl.
- Add melted butter, yogurt, vanilla and grated lemon rind to the mixture and mix well.
- Squeeze lemon juice over baking powder and add to the mixture together with flour. Continue to mix.
- Add the raisons and chopped walnuts. Mix for a further 2 minutes and pour into a greased and floured baking pan.
- Bake at 200 °C for about 30 minutes.

RAISON CAKE
ÜZÜMLÜ KEK

INGREDIENTS

250 g. butter
3 glasses of flour
4 tbsps. yogurt
grated rind of 1 lemon
1/2 tbsp. baking powder
1/2 tbsp. lemon juice
1 packet of vanilla
1 cup of icing sugar

APPLE PIES
ELMALI POĞAÇA

Filling

3 sour cooking apples
1 cup of sugar
1 cup of chopped walnuts
1 tbsp. cinnamon.

COOKING

🍎 Boil the peeled and grated apples with the sugar in a saucepan. Add chopped walnuts and cinnamon.

🍎 In a separate bowl mix the butter, yogurt, lemon rind, vanilla, baking powder and lemon juice together.

🍎 Add the sifted flourand stir untilthe ingredients become a soft dough.

🍎 Take large walnut sized pieces of the dough, shape into rounds (1/2 cm thick) and spread a spoon of the apple + walnut mixture into the center and fold half.

🍎 Place each pie on an oven tray (at 1 cm. intervals). Bake in a moderate oven until golden brown.

🍎 Sift vanilla and icing sugar on top while still hot.

CRISPY SESAME SEED RINGS

TUZLU SİMİT (Serve 10)

INGREDIENTS

250 g. cheese
1 glass of oil
2 eggs
1 glass of yogurt
1 tsp. baking powder
flour
1/2 tbsp. salt

COOKING

- Mix the butter, egg, yogurt and grated cheese in a glass bowl.
- Add and mix the baking powder and flour to the mixture until it becomes a soft dough.
- Taking walnut sized pieces of the dough, form it into rings. Brush each ring with egg-yolk and sprinkle with sesame seeds.
- Place them on a greased baking tray (at 1 cm. intervals) and bake for about 15 minutes in a medium oven.

SAVORY CHEESE PASTRIES
PEYNİRLİ POĞAÇA
(Serves 10)

INGREDIENTS

1 glass of melted butter
1/2 cup of oil
1 glass of yogurt
1 egg
 (seperate white and yolk)
1 tsp. baking powder
juice of 1/4 lemon
1/2 tbsp. salt
flour

Filling:
1/2 bunch of parsley
150 g. cheese

COOKING

❧ Mix oil, yogurt, egg, salt, baking powder and lemon juice in a glass bowl.

❧ Add the flour and then mix well until it becomes a soft dough. Put aside for an hour under a piece of cloth.

❧ Taking walnut sized pieces of the dough, roll out (1 cm. thick) and spread cheese and parsley into the center and fold half.

❧ Place them on a greased oven tray with a space between them.

❧ Brush the tops with egg yolk and sprinkle with sesame seeds.

❧ Bake in a moderate oven.

DILL CAKE (SERVES 10)

DERE OTLU KEK

INGREDIENTS :

4 eggs
1,5 glasses of grated cheese
1 glass of yogurt
1 glass of melted butter
1/4 glass of oil
3-5 glasses of flour
1/2 tbsp. baking powder
1 bunch of dill
1 tsp. salt
1 tbsp black cumin seeds
1 tsp. sesame seeds
juice of 1/2 lemon

COOKING

- Mix eggs, yogurt and butter + oil together in a glass bowl. Set aside 2 tblsp. of the mixture to spread on top later.
- Add grated cheese, dill, baking powder, salt, lemon juice and flour. Mix well.
- Pour the mixture into a greased baking pan. Spread 2 tblsps. of the mixture on top. Sprinkle sesame seeds and black cumin seeds on top.
- Bake in a moderate oven until golden brown.

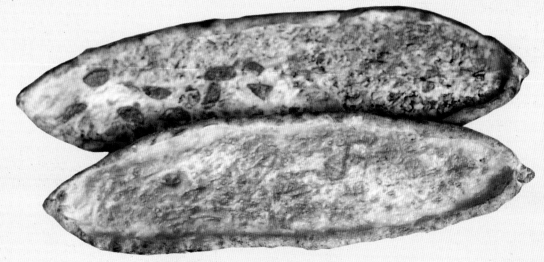

CHEESE PIZZA (Serves 6)
PEYNİRLİ PİDE

INGREDIENTS:

Dough:

500 g. flour
125 g. butter
75 cc. milk
1 tbsp. salt
2 eggs
1 egg (separate white and yolk)
yeast

Filling:

400 g. cheese
1/2 bunch dill + parsley

COOKING

❦ Dissolve the yeast and sugar in the milk. Sift the flour into the mixing bowl and add 2 eggs, butter, and salt. Knead into a soft dough.

❦ Cover the dough and set aside to rise.

❦ Divide the dough into egg-sized pieces. On a floured board flatten each with hands into a circular shape about half a centimeter thick.

❦ Prepare the filling: mix cheese + egg white + dill + parsley and then spread the filling down the center of each piece, about 2 cm. and stretch the pieces lenthwise so that the filling can be seen.

❦ Place them on a greased oven tin. Leave in a warm place to rise again. Brush them with egg-yolk and bake in a moderate oven until they are golden brown.

❦ When cooked, brush lightly with melted butter and place in a covered saucepan for 5 minutes before serving. (it softens the pastry.)

RING-SHAPED CAKE WITH WALNUTS AND GROUND SESAME SEEDS (Serves 8)
CEVİZLİ TAHİNLİ ÇÖREK

INGREDIENTS
500 g. flour
1 tbsp. yeast in powder
(baking powder)
1 egg
1 glass of olive oil
1,5 glass of chopped
walnut
8 tbsp. of tahin
(ground sesame seeds)
salt

COOKING

❧ Add baking powder to 1/2 cup of water and stir. Wait aside until the yeast rises.

❧ Mix flour, salt and the raised yeast in a pan. Add a little water and knead well into a soft dough.

❧ Put the lid on and wait till the dough raises.

❧ Divide the dough into 4 pieces. Roll out each piece 3-4 mm. thick.

❧ Over rolled out pieces, spread olive oil, 2 tbsp. ground sesame seed and chopped walnut.

❧ Roll each piece into thin rolls, twist at the ends. Arrange the twisted rolls into a greased oven tray by rolling up the twisted pieces from the middle to the corners.

❧ Cover the tray and wait until the dough rises.

❧ Beat an egg with 2 tbsp. of olive oil. Spread the mixture over the dough.

❧ Cook in a moderate oven until the top is golden brown.

PS: Immediately after removing from the oven, if you sprinkle 1/2 cup of warm water on top, and if you cover it with a piece of cloth for 15 minutes, it will be softer.

SAVOURY PANCAKES (Serves 6)
GÖZLEME

INGREDIENTS

Dough:
3 glasses flour
2 tbsp. butter
1 tbsp. yogurt
1 tbsp. olive oil
1 tsp. baking powder
5-6 drops of a lemon juice
salt

Filling:
250 g. cheese
1/2 bunch of dill

COOKING

❧ Into a saucepan, put the flour, yogurt, olive oil, salt, baking powder and 5-6 drops of lemon juice. Add a little water and knead well until a soft dough.

❧ Divide the dough into 6 equal pieces, roll out each piece 2 mm. thick. Brush over with melted butter and fold like a small package. Wait for 30 minutes.

❧ Roll out the pieces again 2 mm. thick squares. Onto half put the cheese filling and fold the other half on top. Press the corners by finger.

❧ Then, brown both sides in a pan or over an iron plate.

❧ When it is hot, spread butter on top and serve.

PS:
Minced lamb filling and potato filling can be used in place of cheese filling.

MEASUREMENTS
ÖLÇÜLER

Butter :
1 tbsp: 40 g.

Oil :
1 glass: 200 g.

Flour :
1 glass: 100 g.
1 cup: 30 g.
1 tbsp (full): 15 g.

Semolina :
1 glass: 150 g.
1 cup: 50 g.
1 tbsp (full): 20 g.

Starch :
1 cup: 45 g.

Icing Sugar :
1 glass: 150 g.

Cocoa :
1 tbsp: 15 g.

Sugar :
1 glass: 200 g.
1 cup: 50 g.
1 tbsp: 25 g.

Water :
1 glass: 200 g.

Milk :
1 glass: 220 g.
1 cup: 70 g.

Yogurt :
1 glass: 250 g.

Lentil-chick-peas-white beans:
1 glass: 200 g.

Rice- cracked wheat rice :
1 glass: 220 g.

Walnut-hazelnut-currant-pistachio:
1glass: 75 g.

Yeast :
1 tbsp: 15 g.

Salt :
1/2 tbsp: 20 g.

tsp: teaspoon
tbsp: tablespoon
glass: water glass

124

CW00556885

FLOWER
MARKET

FLOWER MARKET

BOTANICAL STYLE AT HOME

MICHELLE MASON

Pimpernel
Press ltd
www.pimpernelpress.com

SPIRIT CHLORO
DOSE 5-30 MIN.

FRONT COVER
Dried hydrangeas
BACK COVER Peony,
ranunculus and
grape hyacinths
ENDPAPERS
Vintage floral fabric
TITLE PAGE Hydrangeas
fresh from the market
PAGE 2–3 Peony,
ranunculus, pink viburnum
blossom and *Ammi majus*
RIGHT Blue hydrangeas
and green viburnum
in a reclaimed Dutch
tulip bucket

Pimpernel Press Limited
www.pimpernelpress.com

Flower Market:
Botanical Style at Home
Copyright © Pimpernel Press
Limited 2019
Text © Michelle Mason 2019
Photographs © Michelle Mason
2019 except as noted on page 176

Designed by Becky Clarke

Michelle Mason has asserted
her right to be identified as the
author of this book in accordance
with the Copyright, Designs and
Patents Act 1988.

All rights reserved. No part of this
publication may be reproduced,
stored in a retrieval system
or transmitted, in any form,
or by any means, electronic,
mechanical, photocopying,
recording or otherwise, without
prior permission in writing
from the publisher or a licence
permitting restricted copying. In
the United Kingdom such licences
are issued by the Copyright
Licensing Agency, Barnard's Inn,
86 Fetter Lane, London EC4A 1EN.

A catalogue record for this book is
available from the British Library.

Typeset in Playfair and
Linotype Veto

ISBN 978-1-910258-20-0

Printed and bound in China

9 8 7 6 5 4 3 2 1

Contents

About the Author

Michelle Mason, designer and co-owner of vintage emporium Mason & Painter, is passionate about interior design and styling. Known for her strong illustrative style, she has created products for clients including the British Library, Transport for London and House of Fraser. Michelle has worked with some of the UK's most respected manufacturers, from the potteries of Stoke on Trent to Sheffield's last remaining pewter factory. Her own products have regularly appeared in the international design press and she frequently sits on judging panels, such as Boost, launched by the Southbank Centre and *The Observer* to find the next generation of new design talent.

In 2013 Michelle co-founded Mason & Painter lifestyle store on Columbia Road, east London, a street famed for its Sunday flower market, and was immediately invited to create a series of pop-up shops at the Southbank Centre and Kew Gardens. Her interest in styling with flowers and plants is intrinsically linked to the market which each week, unfolds on the doorstep with a huge selection of seasonal plants and flowers.

photo©dvoraphoto

Introduction

The beauty of reclaimed objects holds a constant fascination and, in my career as both a designer and a shopkeeper, I'm continually looking for unusual items, textures and shapes to create combinations that work well together; merging styles and clashing pattern and form. Be it the variety of greens in a crate of fresh garden herbs or the muted surface of an old café table – the search for a look or theme is endlessly captivating.

When the opportunity to open a vintage store came up it seemed like a dream come true as we get to source beautiful age-worn treasure and restore it. One of my favourite aspects has to be spotting a timeless piece and basing a whole look around it, adding a variety of plants or flowers to display alongside our ever-changing selection of vintage glassware and ceramics.

The shop, Mason & Painter, sits on an east London street that was once home to a row of upholstery workshops, serving the booming furniture trade in Shoreditch in the late 1800s. The street is famed for its much-loved flower market and every Sunday is a visual treat as the stalls load up with seasonal plants and flowers.

This regular supply of garden-fresh flowers continuously inspires decoration ideas. I'm tempted by every imaginable plant and flower, colour and shade, from uplifting blue hyacinths in March, peachy peonies and delicate pink foxgloves in June, shades of gold and orange in the autumn, through to pine boughs and jewel-like berries in December.

In *Flower Market: Botanical Style at Home* I share my tips on styling and making the most of seasonal plants and flowers, as well as the work of some of my favourite plant specialists and florists including Conservatory Archives, Rebel Rebel, Grace & Thorn and Aesme Flowers in London. I hope you will find a little botanical inspiration over the following pages and enjoy the images as much as I have enjoyed putting them together.

WHY FLOWER MARKET?

Today's consumers are increasingly mindful of the origins of merchandise and are regularly opting to buy fairtrade or organically grown – preferring local and fresh to mass-produced, mass-farmed products. This trend not only cuts back on the carbon footprint, it also supports community markets and small independent traders.

On my doorstep every Sunday I see customers experience the pleasure of buying flowers directly from the grower or trader to be carried, wrapped in paper, back home. The appeal is the story behind the encounter and the pleasure of decorating a corner of a room with fresh flowers.

Inspiration by Season

Working with seasonal flowers has to be one of the most rewarding and exciting aspects for a florist, as every calendar month brings a stunning variety of shape and colour. At the start of the year January blooms with brilliant blue grape hyacinths, pretty snowdrops, mimosa and gorse; February brings winter jasmine, crocus, anemones and calla lilies. Spring bursts into life with a treasure trove of gems including boughs of blossom, daffodils, ranunculus, camellias, anemones and, later in the season, some of my all-time favourites: bluebells, sweet peas and lilacs.

Early summer follows with gorgeous white lilac, foxgloves and peonies. Summer show-stoppers include blowsy peonies, roses, foxgloves and lupins and as the season unfurls through the warmer months of June, July and August the variety of flowers and foliage reaches its most glorious peak. This is, no doubt, the most productive and creative time for growers and florists as they prepare for summer weddings and other events.

ABOVE Autumn colour with ripening fruit, dahlias, late roses and foliage
RIGHT An emerald glazed confit pot with fresh summer greens including guelder rose (*Viburnum opulus*) leaves, cow parsley, lemony lupins, blush pink foxgloves and cream foxgloves with dark chocolate centres.

We generally think of autumn as a golden harvest with the arrival of physalis – the orange Chinese lantern plant – saffron-coloured dahlias, lemony daisy-like helianthus and pumpkins in time for Halloween.

As winter beds in we decorate our homes with evergreens and berries and hardy flowering shrubs such as viburnum, with its pretty pink and white flowers, and sprigs of pale yellow winter-flowering chimonanthus.

In the following pages I have highlighted different flowers and plants, showing what to look out for as each season unfolds and how they can be styled and arranged at home.

ABOVE A pretty hand-tied bouquet with zinnia, pheasant bush, roses, calendula, grasses, scabious, little crab apples, chocolate cosmos and clematis by Aesme Flowers, London.
LEFT A vintage floral wall chart is displayed with ferns planted in reclaimed biscuit tins.

Spring

After the cold winter months it's always a joy to welcome early spring blooms such as hyacinths, heady with perfume and colour, golden daffodiles and fragrant paperwhite narcissi. Fragile snowdrops, tiny grape hyacinths, crocus and lily of the valley also brave the chill and woodlands gleam with yellow celandines, wild primroses and bluebells in April and early May. Hedgerows sparkle with hawthorn, pretty blackthorn and hazel catkins. Spring arrives at the flower market as early as February with stalls of tulips, potted primroses, bulbs ready to bud and branches of blackthorn, apple and magnolia.

LEFT Pretty pinks, as parks and gardens fill with magnolia blossom at the end of March and early April.

This palette of spring colour, randomly arranged on a metal bistro table (left), includes soft pink primroses, tulips, grape hyacinths, orange ranunculus, yellow and blue hyacinths, cream freesia, snowdrops and white wax flower.

Try adding colour interest and height to your displays by planting or grouping flowers in a variety of containers. Here I used a selection of reclaimed plant pots, jars, bottles, a vintage coffee tin and an old red champagne bucket picked up at a boot fair.

Sparkling pots of spring colour look lovely displayed indoors. The grape hyacinths shown above have been planted with clumps of moss for extra greenery. These, together with primroses and daffodils, can be enjoyed for a good few weeks. Pinch away any dead flower heads and keep the soil moist by watering regularly.

I love to use branches of delicate cherry and apple blossom in the shop. For me, these blossoms, along with pussy willow, pollen-heavy catkins and magnolia flowers, mark the true arrival of spring.

ABOVE April cherry blossom
LEFT A single arch of magnolia blossom with a vintage fruit crate and dark green glass set against an inky blue wall.

For an uplifting early spring treat there's nothing like a pot of fragrant paperwhites on a windowsill. Hyacinths also appear early in the season, closely followed by white, gold and pink tulips. In April and May the larger peony-like, fuller-flowered tulip varieties come on to the market in a blaze of colour from scorching hot reds to ballet-slipper pinks, yellows and ivory streaked with peach. For pots and tubs look out for violas; I particularly like the pretty little Sorbet violas and the lemony, lilac and cream Bel Viso varieties planted with white-flowered *Saxifraga* 'Apple Blossom'.

Spring colour at the flower market, with boxes jam-packed with hyacinths and tulips.

As late spring turns to summer lilac spreads its glorious colour across parks and gardens. Its cone-shaped blooms, consisting of a mass of tiny flowers, range from white through to pastel mauve, violet and deep crimson and its perfume is sweet and fragrant.

It's a popular cut flower for spring boquets or, as shown here, it is delicious on its own with just a flourish of cow parsley and pale green viburnum. Other late-spring flowers include aquilegia, with its dove-like winged petals, the zingy lime-yellow spurge *Euphorbia polychroma*, and sweet-smelling stocks that come in a delightful palette range of cream, peach, soft pink and damson.

ABOVE Lilac appears in parks and gardens from early May.
LEFT Here lilac is arranged in a simple ceramic vase.

Summer

Beautiful, sweet-smelling peonies seem the quintessential choice for summer blooms. They range from the ruffle-feathered pink blush variety 'Sarah Bernhardt' to the deep burgundy 'Rubra Plena' and the white 'Alba Plena', all of which have large velvety double flowers. 'Coral Sunset', a little less full-flowered but equally pretty, with a gold and apricot centre, reminds me of my grandmother's garden. Shown opposite in a Victorian tea caddy is a selection of pale, full-flowered 'Sarah Bernhardt' peonies, deep pink ranunculus, white and rose-pink viburnum, lilacs and green moluccella, sometimes known as bells of Ireland. Take care to avoid the long sharp spikes when handling the moluccella stems.

As we reach May and June the flower market comes alive with colour and variety, ranging from peonies the size of saucers to roses in every shape and shade; exotic oriental poppies, delphiniums, cornflowers, phlox, pear-scented snapdragons and so many dainty and delicate meadow flowers such as forget-me-nots, fennel and mustard flowers. A little later in the season these are followed by bee-loving hollyhocks, 'butterfly-blue' scabious, feverfew and calendula. The choice is overwhelming.

ABOVE Horse chestnut tree blossom in May
RIGHT An early summer picnic surrounded by apple blossom, with pitchers of peonies, parrot tulips and ranunculus, and forget-me-nots in a little blue bottle.

There's something magical about warm summer evenings and spending time outdoors as the days grow longer. Eating al fresco or inviting friends round for drinks is the best part, especially if you make the setting a little extra special by adding a handful of flowers. If you don't have a garden or balcony, a lazy picnic in the park is just as good and little bunches of sweet peas in portable jam jars or a tendril of honeysuckle with white cosmos will add to the sunniness.

ABOVE This simple posy using mint, strawberry leaf and a geranium flower makes a lovely addition to an outdoor table set with vintage plates.
LEFT White anemones with lemony goldenrod

Heritage flowers such as forget-me-nots, trailing honeysuckle, wild sweet briar, lily-of-the-valley (symbolizing happiness), lupins, larkspur and foxgloves make dreamy summer bouquets and add unusual elements to wedding flowers.

ABOVE Sweet peas and a peony flanked by a home-grown strawberry and a snippet of cow parsley.
LEFT Washed linens and pale, worn cooking pots, simply decorated with 'Coral Sunset' peonies and green viburnum.
OVERLEAF London parks fill with colour: horse chestnut trees in full bloom

Autumn

Autumn, the time of year for kicking through crisp, fallen leaves in the park, and the season when fruit and berries ripen to golden, coppery tones, reds and russets. Bronze-coloured dahlias start to appear on the market at the end of September together with asters and zinnias. Gleaming sunflowers and heleniums, with their streaks of gold, buttery Jamaican primroses and echinacea daisies are now in season too and look good as cut flowers or planted in pots and tubs.

LEFT Sprigs of pink snowberries with eucalyptus in a vintage silver coffee pot, and a single blush hydrangea.
BELOW Autumn fruits: squash, figs and sweet chestnuts with hydrangeas and snowberries for display.

When the warmer days of September and early October have passed, along with the colourful flowers of late summer, we start to see varieties with autumnal tones such as chocolate cosmos, flame-coloured crocosmia 'Lucifer', physalis, late dahlias, rose hips, poppy heads, all manner of berries, jewel-like crab apples still on the branch and *Rudbeckia hirta*, sometimes known as black-eyed Susan.

ABOVE An assortment of pumpkins, squash and gourds outside a grocery store in east London
LEFT An autumn posy arranged in a vintage French preserve jar with rose, cream, burgundy and saffron-coloured dahlias and little apple serviceberries.
OVERLEAF Autumn posies with a selection of ranunculus, asters, amaryllis, crocosmia and an Icelandic poppy

The harvesting of marrows, squash and pumpkins is a reminder of Halloween and in the UK of Bonfire Night, and a great excuse to decorate our homes with carved lanterns. The last of the roses are picked, as are the dark, chocolatey purple 'Velvet Noir' hydrangeas, gerberas and gladioli, which feature in the floral installation, above, by American florist Katie Davis at Ponderosa and Thyme, when she visited Columbia Road.

RIGHT I love the gangly grace of these physalis (Chinese lanterns) as they turn from yellow to orange and dark sepia.

Autumn is also a stunning time of the year in the parks, woodlands and countryside, when deciduous trees slowly give way to an autumn rainbow of red, amber, ochre and the colour of burnt caramel. I love foraging in London Fields, shown left, close to the flower market in London's east end, for conkers, acorns, blackberries and fallen leaves to use in flower arrangements.

Sparky autumn colour inspired this collection of little posies. These mini arrangements, in vintage bottles and ceramics, make perfect seasonal table settings for gatherings such as Bonfire Night or Thanksgiving. I used a combination of vibrant hues to include yellowy sycamore leaves, fiery crocosmia

'Lucifer', burgundy amaryllis, honey-coloured and copper-tipped ranunculus, champagne anemones, goldenrod (solidago), orange and white pumpkins, lemony quince, amber asters, copper yew twigs and russet pears grouped with a little bronze watering can and a stack of vintage linen-bound cookery books.

Winter

As the winter chill sets in and the days become shorter I look forward to seeing the first branches of spruce, fir and pine arrive at the Sunday flower market with their verdant, woody aromas – for me it marks the start of the season.

LEFT A pale winter arrangement with cream stoneware, a dahlia and little apple serviceberries.
BELOW A posy of dried flowers including nigella, peony, grasses and hydrangea from Grace & Thorn, London. For tips on drying flowers see page 171.
OVERLEAF A small bunch of hellebores with fir cones, a fir branch and ivy for a winter table setting.

Lipstick red amaryllis fire up this festive table-setting with evergreens, and a posy of hellebores, rosemary and sage. Fruit and flowers are laid out amongst vintage plates and glassware along with an old miner's lamp.

The pagan custom of bringing in the yule log or seasonal branch dates back centuries in northern European countries and was centred on the mid-winter feast.

ABOVE Peachy-coloured ranunculus

I love the simplicity of tied bundles of pine that come on to the market from early December and I often buy armfuls of eucalyptus to fill the shop with its fresh, uplifting fragrance. For variety try teaming round-leaved eucalyptus with the smaller flat-leaved *Eucalyptus parvifolia* and add white snowberries, myrtle and, if you can find it, old man's beard (*Clematis vitalba*).

Winter florals needn't be limited to evergreens and dried leaves. November still offers little sparkles of colour like these caramel-coloured ranunculus, anemones and rosy apricot, peach and yellow late-flowering Iceland poppies. In this simple grouping I left the stems long and placed the flowers in a wide-necked jar with a 5 litre (1 gallon) capacity.

Inspiration by Colour

I am obsessed with colour. It's a constant can't-leave-it-alone passion and in my role as shopkeeper/stylist I'm continually playing with combinations to create colours that work well together, blending palettes and building layers of hue and texture, which might come from the the coloured spines in a stack of old books or the way a wall of graffiti changes with passing light. The depth and range of colour is endlessly inspiring.

My favourite labour of love has to be putting a look together using a variety of plants and flowers to bring the market indoors. Here, I've grouped ideas by colour to illustrate some favourite combinations and different style ideas for interiors or small gardens, and created planted containers using vintage finds and repurposed items in unexpected ways.

In the following pages I look at using flowers and plants from several different colour groups, ranging from soft, muted creams and whites, through colour-pop brights, warm pinks and oranges to the cooler tones of blue and green. I place them in a variety of locations; some dark and moody, others light and feminine.

This is a walk-through of examples, rather than a comprehensive list; the real pleasure here is taking inspiration from flowers and foliage as they become seasonably available, and creating a palette within a complementary setting.

Whatever the season, I like to start by unwrapping flowers and laying them out on a table. For a natural organic feel experiment with different combinations, letting the colours work their own magic.

LEFT Pastel Parma violet shades with pretty aquilegia, pink sweet peas, nigella and creamy vintage lace at the window.
OVERLEAF Spring greens, pinks and soft lilacs

Emerald • Verdigris • Evergreen

Soft green vintage preserve jars, tarnished copper cooking pots, succulents, trailing ivy, waxy eucalyptus, the dark green of foxglove leaves, branches of woody spruce and scented herbs all inspired the images here.

Copper is a lovely metal to work with; its warm soft red tone sits beautifully with green, as does the metal's gorgeous green verdigris tarnish, as found on these copper cooking vats, left.

If you have outdoor space you could try a planter such as this reclaimed galvanized metal water tank, above. Salvaged troughs, buckets and washtubs all look good planted with ferns, leafy hostas, olive and bay trees.

A variety of succulents grouped together is instantly uplifting and easy to look after. Try planting them in vintage biscuit tins, reclaimed terracotta plant pots or old seed trays for a more unusual look.

You'll need to drive several drainage holes through the base of outdoor planters and tubs, before planting up, to prevent waterlogging.

OPPOSITE, TOP, LEFT TO RIGHT Green viburnum; succulents; water melons
OPPOSITE, BOTTOM Ripening cherries in a small bottle, displayed on a stack of vintage books.

GARDEN FLOWERS

BRITISH BUTTERFLIES

London's Barbican Centre boasts the second largest conservatory of its kind in London. It houses over 1,500 species within a purpose-built rooftop glasshouse. Even though it is so big, many of the ideas and plants used here translate easily to a domestic setting.

ABOVE A weeping fig tree and banana palms within the conservatory, and luscious tropical greenery, **RIGHT** Kentia palms and windmill palms, both of which are easy to grow and care for at home in tubs.

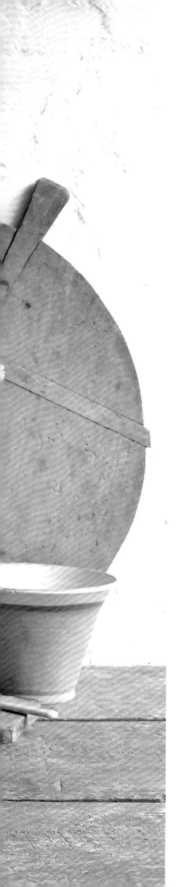

Cornflower • Cobalt • Indigo

I love the colour combination, above, of the fading delphiniums, the summery white and lilac-blue hydrangea and the delft blue ceramics mixed with the steely metal surface. The galvanized container was originally used to collect olives during harvest time and makes an ideal planter for the white viburnum.

LEFT Clusters of pompom-like green viburnum flowers appear in late April and early May and look bright and fresh with the large-flowered blue hydrangea. They are shown here in a vintage Dutch tulip bucket.

Hyacinths are sold as cut flowers at the flower market. A bunch can last a couple of weeks if the water is kept fresh. I use any small container to hold several stems and enjoy seeing the flowers flop into interesting shapes as they bloom and grow top-heavy.

RIGHT Startling blue cornflowers are displayed here in mismatched glass bottles
BELOW LEFT A vintage dairy bowl holds bunches of ultramarine hyacinths, adding a shot of glorious inky colour to a pale interior.
BELOW RIGHT Small posies for table settings with blue hyacinths, purple stocks and eucalyptus
OPPOSITE Pastel-coloured flowers such as these small peony ranunculus opposite, look pretty against the pale denim walls.

I chose flowers to echo the soft muted blues and pinks of the vintage maps on the wall. The pale blue hyacinths, delphiniums, white wax flowers and pink astrantia are arranged in a selection of French sugar tins and blue and green vintage bottles.

Tangerine • Peach • Saffron

When I think of summer it is invariably sunny Mediterranean holidays that come to mind. Childhood trips to Spain often involved visiting La Boqueria food market on Barcelona's Las Ramblas to buy sun-kissed peaches, nectarines and apricots, the warm saffron colours reflecting the heat of the Spanish sun.

For the photograph above I used a large amber preserve jar as the starting point, its colour reminiscent of barley sugar, and added summer fruit, vintage cooking pots and a peachy linen tablecloth for a welcoming breakfast setting.

Grouping similar colours, left, is a little trick I use in the shop. It has a way of drawing the eye and can bring a look together. I used the oil painting of blowsy summer roses, picked up for pennies at a vintage market, to set the tone. The soft peachy pink of the flowers is echoed in the summer fruit displayed in a vintage French jam jar and stacked on a shelf of books with red and orange cloth spines.

If you're looking for warm peachy tones, try peony ranunculus, like the ones shown here, with hints of caramel, saffron, tea rose and melon. Autumn dahlias also offer a similar palette, with beautiful warm tones from café au lait to vibrant tangerine. And for a delicate orange sorbet feel, look out for zinnias, apricot calla lilies, gerberas, roses, snapdragons or Iceland poppies.

LEFT Peachy foxgloves, tangerine- and yellow-coloured gerberas, butterfly ranunculus tinged with caramel and sweet peas in a 'coffee pot' vase.

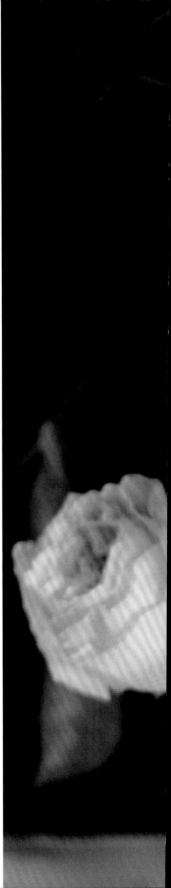

I love the scent of early summer stocks and the gorgeous apricot variety I used here filled the entire room with a sweet clove-like fragrance. Using an old glass jar I added white anenomes, coral pink freesia, zesty ranunculus and a peach tea rose for a romantic English garden feel and set it against a vintage botanical wall chart with illustrations of sweet peas.

This little scene was inspired by flower paintings from the Dutch Golden Age of the late 1600s, when still-life paintings depicting exotic botanicals became popular.

FINDING INSPIRATION

Dutch Old Master flower painters such as Jan van Huysum (1682–1749), Rachel Ruysch (1664–1750) and Ambrosius Bosschaert (1573–1621) were influenced by the emergence of horticulture in the Netherlands and the new exotics available to them such as hyacinths from Asia, pineapples from South America and the highly prized tulip from Turkey.

Many of today's florists and flower artists look towards these dramatic paintings for inspiration; setting their work against dark interiors for added impact, and using flowers that include heritage varieties as well as unusual botanicals such as herbs, vines and grasses.

ABOVE Inspiration from a postcard from the National Gallery, London, showing *Still Life of Flowers in a Wan-Li Vase* (1609–10) by Ambrosius Bosschaert.
LEFT Fiery orange and yellow tulips with chemists' bottles, a conch shell and a botanical wall chart.

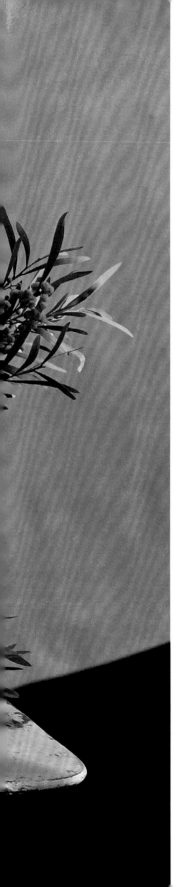

Yellow • Gold • Citrus

Yellow, the colour we relate to sunshine; meadow flowers such as buttercups and marigolds; golden sunflowers, canary yellow ranunculus and the uplifting hue of citrus fruits – yellow is the perfect summer-tinged pick-me-up.

I like to add yellow accents such as this vase of sweet mimosa (left) or a jar of lemons (above) for an instant fix. Yellow is a lovely colour to work with and combines well with earthy terracotta, charcoal and dark green, orange, teal and dark blue.

For a welcoming shot of yellow look out for golden Welsh poppies, pale yellow peonies, the lemony drizzle of snapdragons and late summer's sun-kissed *Coreopsis tinctoria*, shown in a vintage tub with mustard glazed pots and an amber glass jar (right).

I love experimenting with accent colours such as the bold citrusy wall paint, above. Dried poppy heads, a brass desk lamp and a blue star fern add a touch of bohemian elegance to the brightly coloured workspace.

Rose • Soft Pink • Blush

'Pink is the navy blue of India', so said Diana Vreeland, the legendary editor of US *Vogue*. It's certainly not a colour for the faint-hearted but in the natural world softer shades of pink can look refreshing, playful and crisp.

Coral, pale rose, blossom, lychee, shell and blush; these subtle pink tones go so well with stronger colours such as warm gold, saffron, amber and bronze.

This little posy of peachy pink Dutch stocks, anemones, sweet peas, butterfly ranunculus – with a floaty delicate petal – and pink-tinged eucalyptus leaf has a romantic spring feel. Perfect for a table set for tea with a vintage fabric tablecloth.

Soft pinks can look fresh and pretty combined with other pastel colours such as pistachio green, lemon, sky blue and vanilla. Try grouping with different coloured vases or add weight with elements of glass and metal.

The rose-like camellia blossoms in springtime, along with magnolia and cherry; its graceful petals ranging from palest blush pink to bright fuchsia. Try a single stem in a small jar or an old perfume bottle for an instant pop of charm.

Pale salmon pink and ivory roses, mauve, white and violet anemones and sprigs of rosemary take centre stage on my kitchen table.

Cream • Flax • Ivory

Using vintage fabrics is a great way to layer pattern and colour and I especially like to use neutral fabrics such as hessian, hemp and plain linens to add tone and texture, such as the flax sugar sack, shown right. The worn, faded cloth, stamped with the company's logo, makes an attractive wall graphic and backdrop to the pale floral arrangement of white lilac, tulips with honey-coloured centres, cream narcissi and palest pink viburnum.

ABOVE White horse chestnut blossom

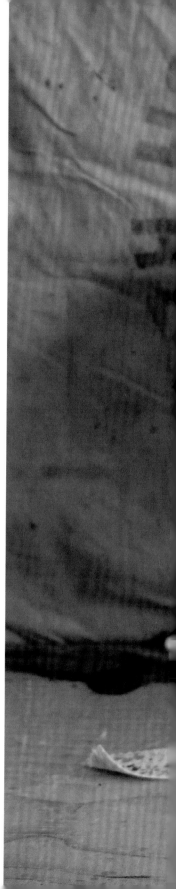

When styling areas of the shop I usually have a theme or narrative in mind relating to the objects we bring in. Vintage pieces are frequently passed on with their own story, although very occasionally we know little about the object's history, its previous owner or where it came from.

Flowers sometimes come with stories too: about where they were grown or how they were nurtured by the grower from heritage seeds. Part of the pleasure for me is inventing my own stories and for this display I thought about the colour cream. It's a quiet colour, calm and often associated with a feeling of nostalgia and history.

After putting the flowers together I added a group of books for texture. The effect of the pale, coverless books and romantic cream flowers reminded me of the women connected to the Bloomsbury Group and their beautiful gardens in the south of England in the early twentieth century.

ABOVE Cream dahlia
LEFT Referencing Virginia Woolf's *A Room of One's Own*, with journals, old keys, and a fragrant posy of vanilla sweet peas, oat grass, mint, strawberry leaves, cream and lilac anemones and a creamy blush rose.

This botanical illustration from the 1920s sets the background tone for a delicately faded scene (right) . The caramel-coloured rose was the starting point for the flowers and I added the fragrant cream double daffodils with a buttery yellow centre, aptly named 'Cheerfulness', with hazel twigs, white freesia and pearly butterfly ranunculus.

Cream is a colour often associated with purity, peace and serenity. Traditionally in the West it's a popular colour choice for bridal dresses and bouquets. Look out for other cream or ivory flowers throughout the year such as allium, lilies, orchids, dahlias, white cornflowers (*Centaurea*), cosmos, daisies, white bluebells, nigella, iris, white briar and hawthorn blossom.

ABOVE White foxgloves

Burnt Orange • Russet • Pomegranate

Single stems of ranunculus daubed with the warm spicy tones of turmeric, ginger and russet, together with these fiery orange Parrot tulips, streaked with green and burgundy, add delicious splashes of colour to the little stack of books. The tiny bottles, the tobacco tin, the terracotta inkpot and the beautifully worn cricket balls, enveloped in scarlet leather, also found their way on to the table overleaf.

Grouping old books by colour is a great way to display their cloth spines and makes an interesting backdrop to a desk or bookshelf. Look out for eye-catching second-hand books in thrift shops and place a stack of them under a jar of flowers or alongside your pot plants.

These lovely dove grey shutters make a great neutral backdrop to the glorious burnt orange poppies, stripy radish-coloured anemones, with blossoming blackthorn, butterscotch ranunculus, a sprig of fresh greenery and maidenhair fern.

Decoration & Display at Home

I love to pore over the latest homes and gardens magazines and sometimes wonder what it would be like to have a large flower garden or spacious home. I live in a typical London apartment: a compact, brick-built, Victorian top floor flat with a tiny roof terrace. It's small but it's my sanctuary and it's all about being practical and resourceful, especially if space is limited.

Creating a Look

There is nothing more inspiring than a quick refresh. This can be achieved quickly and relatively easily by creating a space for house plants, fresh flowers, plus a little imagination and some cherished pots, vases or containers. Whether you're aiming for a subtle update or something a little more dramatic this chapter offers tips on how to work with plants and flowers at home, and styling ideas using salvaged items and junk shop finds.

For a classic, timeless look you need to get the balance right between what works for your individual style, the way it looks in your home and your budget. Our individual style comes together organically over time, as our tastes and preferences develop.

The hallway or foot of the stairs is an area often overlooked; it can quickly turn into a space for dumping shopping bags, bicycles, shoes . . . but it's usually the first area of the home you see as you walk through the front door. Add some interest with a leafy plant or two, a welcoming vase of fresh flowers or, as shown opposite, a little arrangement of books, a potted hydrangea and a vintage ceramic dairy bowl. Below, a metal cabinet hides shoes and school bags and a simple jar of forsythia adds a subtle homespun charm.

TOP LEFT A vintage dairy bowl is used to store artichokes.
BOTTOM LEFT A bookshelf with old French pharmacy bottles and succulents
RIGHT Forsythia in a vintage preserve jar
OVERLEAF An arch of green viburnum with 'Coral Sunset' peonies and apricot-coloured foxgloves displayed with old cooking pots and wooden boards.

Styling with Ceramics, Glass, Metal & Reclaimed Objects

When our little shop on Columbia Road first opened little did we know that we'd expand after the first year and move across the street to an old upholstery workshop. With more floor space and a small backyard we were now able to stock the kind of items that felt right for visitors to the flower market as well as larger salvaged objects that our existing customers hankered after.

They loved the large 8-, 10- and 15-litre vintage preserve jars for flowers. They wanted original washtubs for olive trees and Japanese maples. They asked for galvanized metal troughs and reclaimed water tanks and landscape gardeners sought out unconventional items for their clients' gardens.

ABOVE A selection of glass jars and a geranium planted in an old paint kettle.
LEFT A collection of 1960s and 1970s studio pottery with vintage eastern European hand-thrown pots. These look equally good arranged as a collection or used individually to display flowers and foliage.

We use a variety of ceramics and terracotta in the shop – anything from Victorian plant pots to cast-off cooking vessels – their worn surfaces and textures look fabulous with flowers and greenery. Look out for old flour bins, casserole dishes and baking trays at vintage fairs and thrift shops – all look beautiful when planted up.

Yellow and green glazed *confit* pots (above) were commonly used in France to cook duck or goose. The pots were then buried up to the glazed line in cool cellars to preserve the *confit* in the days before refrigeration.

ABOVE Elegantly arched love-lies-bleeding and poppy heads in a green-glazed pot
LEFT Terracotta pots, still caked in earth, displayed with a staghorn fern and an old pair of leather boots echoing the same warm, earthy tones.

Adding a little floral decoration at home needn't take up lots of time or cost the earth, if anything at all. A little bit of imagination and resourcefulness and you can create small posies, single stem arrangements and interesting looks with cuttings in jars, recycled glass bottles, even a pretty drinking glass from your kitchen cupboard.

Experiment with fallen leaves and twigs from the park, cuttings from a friend's garden or allotment, shoots from potted plants, flowers from the market or window box herbs. Anything goes.

A large dark green bottle, left, once used for the manufacture of spirits, is the same emerald green as the monstera plant and large stag horn fern, in a sunny corner by a window.

Vintage glass preserve jars, overleaf, old chemists' bottles with gilt lettering, cloudy old lemonade and beer bottles, medicine bottles, olive oil and wine flagons – the effect of mixing different textures, sizes and colours can look fresh and elegant when grouped and simply styled with leaves and flowers.

Little posies of peony ranunculus, pink viburnum blossom and *Ammi majus* (a form of cow parsley sometimes known as bishop's flower) in a collection of glassware from cloudy *eau de vie* bottles, chemists' bottles, inkpots and an old jam jar.

If you enjoy collecting reclaimed ceramics, plant pots or metal containers chances are you're already using them as planters. I personally can't resist the graphics and typography on old tubs, tins and boxes and have a least a dozen planted up with succulents, ferns, hostas or spring bulbs at any one time.

Metal tubs can easily be picked up from junk shops and antique fairs and make great outdoor and indoor planters. To guarantee good drainage it's good practice to drill or hammer several holes in the base before planting. Galvanized buckets, troughs, water tanks, food tins and olive harvest baskets make ideal containers. These look great teamed with vintage metal garden furniture – ours have often come from old French cafés – complete with several layers of paint and faded sherbet colours they create a lovely setting for patio plants and serve as a reminder of sunny Riviera holidays.

The copper pots, pictured,
were once used to cook
over open fires and have an
interesting combination of
dark, smoky colours and green
verdigris tarnish. Galvanized
buckets with handles make
fantastic hanging planters.

Plants & Flowers at Home

For this next chapter I visit three very different homes. Although all the owners have a common interest in plants and flowers, my main draw is the individuality of the properties and the way each home is styled to create a unique living space. The three properties featured include a town house with a bamboo garden, a vibrant London house with a love of colour and flowers and a loft-style, open-plan apartment with a roof terrace,

Plants in the Home

This east London home is an exemplary lesson in comfort and style. Calming greens, cool greys and colour-pop mustards run throughout the three-bedroomed Edwardian terraced house just a stone's throw from the green space of London Fields.

It helps that owners Paul and Philip have an intuitive talent for spotting classic design pieces such as the Robin Day sofa, collectable Eames chairs and vintage Polish poster art. House plants feature throughout their home and the super-stylish back garden is lavishly planted with tree ferns and sky-high bamboo.

ABOVE The dining room opens out on to the garden planted with bamboo and tree ferns.
RIGHT An asparagus fern in the study

Paul built the sunken garden to encompass a decked, shady oasis of tropical palms and lush greens. Borders planted with bamboo, tree ferns, castor oil plants and Cornish ferns surround a central fire pit. Pots of bonsai Japanese maple are dotted around the edges and on the outdoor dining table and the overall view from the kitchen is one of complete calm and serenity.

Flowers in the Home

This family home in Hackney, east London, is full of fun and colour and is a tribute to its owners, Charlotte (a designer of children's clothes and home accessories) and jeweller Ben, who live there with their children, Dorian and Gracie, and Daisy the dog.

Charlotte and Ben's love of colour, typography and popular culture is evident throughout the house, and their collection of whimsical graphics, film posters and vintage fabrics is supplemented with greenery and flowers in every room.

ABOVE In a corner of the living room a yellow and pink colour combination positively sizzles against the dark grey wall and smoky velvet sofa. The over-sized fuchsia table lamp sits on a sulphur yellow coffee table with a jug of soft pink roses and basket weave vessels.
RIGHT A jar of multi-coloured anemones on top of the piano surrounded by colourful graphics and family photographs.

Cacti, palms and flowers blend seamlessly into the bright open plan living space where floor-to-ceiling glass doors lead out to a small back garden filled with tubs and planters.

The encaustic floor tiles in the kitchen were custom-made in Mexico to Charlotte's specification. The candy colours extend throughout the ground floor, with a cool mint green central island and deckchair stripe fabrics to create a fresh al fresco feeling.

LEFT Red and white tulips, daisies and a tall desert torch cactus in the early morning light
RIGHT A dragon tree (*Dracaena marginata*) in the bathroom

Cacti & Succulents in the Home

With impressive views of Canary Wharf on one side and the City of London to the west, this light-filled warehouse conversion is located in a vast former dog biscuit factory, originally built in 1899. Carol, the owner of the apartment, is a make-up artist and ceramicist and the pots she creates are often sold ready-planted with succulents and cacti.

As Carol frequently travels for work she has filled her live-work space with low maintenance plants such as the succulent *Euphorbia* 'Cowboy', trailing ripsalis, ficus and prickly pear cacti.

RIGHT Plants are stylishly planted in wooden and cast-iron bowls and placed on the floor of the apartment.

Carol's pots, above, with their brightly-coloured glazes are neatly stacked and ready to send out to customers.

The large open-plan living area, on the previous page, is separated from the workspace by a low-level divider, left, filled with various cacti and succulents, spider plants, aloe vera and the small awl cactus sometimes known as Eve's needle.

Beside my Victorian fireplace: a monstera, commonly known as a Swiss cheese plant; on the far left is a fiddle-leaf fig. On the mantlepiece, from left to right, a pilea with flat leaves like little pancakes; a ghost plant and money tree succulent and a string of hearts.

Living with House Plants

My small rooftop deck has just enough space for a handful of plants in pots and several chairs. I think myself lucky to have this little oasis in central London. The trouble is that I love greenery and my expanding urban jungle inevitably spills into the living room and kitchen – I see this as my little indoor garden and enjoy adding to it every now and then. In this chapter I share examples of how to display a variety of house plants with information about how I look after them.

You don't need much room to create an indoor green space or enjoy a random plant or two. Fortunately many house plants will happily sit on a sunny windowsill. If you're starting from scratch try grouping a few low-maintenance succulents, cacti or spider plants on a sun-lit shelf or bookcase.

For larger indoor areas you could try a mixed collection of plants on a console table or old desk; try hanging trailing varieties from the ceiling or arrange leafy plants of differing heights in an unused fireplace. I bought this selection from the weekly flower market, although any garden centre or flower shop is likely to stock similar.

FROM LEFT TO RIGHT: A trailing ivy hangs from the ceiling; below it sits an asparagus fern planted in an old biscuit tin, a prickly desert cactus (*pilocereus*), a small ivy, a money tree (*Crassula ovata*), pink jelly bean succulents (sedums), a dieffenbachia with variegated foliage in an old paint kettle, a dark green aloe plant in a vintage terracotta pot and a staghorn fern (*Platycerium bifurcatum*) suspended from the ceiling.

My open-plan living area has an old French café table at the foot of the stairs where, positioned opposite a sunny window, it makes an ideal console for houseplants. Shown here is a stringy pencil cactus, a succulent *Crassula ovata* 'Gollum' and a trailing ivy, a tiny money tree and a hanging fishbone cactus (which is actually a succulent), with its whimsical zigzag foliage.

OVERLEAF, LEFT TO RIGHT Sweet broom, violas 'Heartsease' and 'Sorbet Lemon', yellow peony ranunculus, geranium 'Veronica Contreras', strawberry plant, butterfly ranunculus, spider plant and white saxifraga

Pictured here and overleaf is the interior of Conservatory Archives, formerly the location of London's oldest ironmongers. As the name suggests, it resembles a repository from a bygone era, with its unique features including exposed walls, worn flooring and the original trolley slope to the warehouse below. The building now houses an extensive and impressive collection of plants and sits like an emerald treasure trove on Hackney Road in east London.

Foliage and fronds trail down the walls, flow from the high ceilings or grow from tubs and pots placed on the floor. Rubber plants (*Ficus elastica*), elephant ear (*Alocasia*) and a bird of paradise plant (*Strelitzia reginae*) surround a leather chair (opposite).

If you have floor space at home you could try a potted tropical plant such as a leafy banana or Kentia palm – all look beautifully exotic and are relatively easy to care for (see overleaf). If space is tight try potted cacti or a string of pearls succulent to dangle from a door fame or place on a bedroom shelf.

ABOVE A potted peace lily, snake plant (*Sansevieria*) and mature *Heteropanax* tree at Conservatory Archives

EASY-CARE HOUSE PLANTS

Ferns happily live indoors year-round and make lovely house plants. You could try the easy-to-care-for Boston fern (good for removing air pollutants), asparagus fern, maidenhair fern or the bird's nest fern with its long crimped-edge leaves. All are naturally suited to shady habitats and are ideally suited to the damp conditions of bathrooms. Mist their leaves on a regular basis, keep the surface soil moist but not sodden and place your fern away from direct sunlight; soft, dappled light is ideal. Spider plants make great house plants too and look good suspended in macramé hangers. I have mine next to a large fishbone cactus and water both plants every couple of weeks, misting their leaves between watering.

Large-leaved plants such as the banana, fiddle-leaf fig and monstera like a warm environment. Position them in a light spot but avoid harsh, direct sunlight. Keep the soil moist in summer and feed with houseplant food once a month. Reduce watering in winter to prevent waterlogging.

Cacti naturally live in arid desert conditions and only need watering when the soil becomes dry; let any excess water drain away into the sink or a saucer, never leave the soil over saturated

The stag horn fern grows best when the soil is allowed to dry out between watering and likes a cool shady spot; mine appreciates a little misting weekly and enjoys the cooler area at the back of the shop.

Pilea and string of hearts need only small amounts of water and grow best in a sunny position avoiding direct-all-day sun.Let the surface soil dry out between waterings.

Fleshy succulents, such as aloes, sedums and crassula naturally store water in their leaves and can go for a couple of weeks without watering. Water moderately when the soil becomes dry and more frequently in the summer.

Arranging Flowers at Home

Whether it's putting flowers together for the shop, the kitchen table or to style a photograph the experience is always a treat and a pleasure that I tend to approach as I would an illustration or painting; starting with an idea, then choosing a colour palette and lastly checking what's available at the flower market or my local flower shop. I studied art and design, not floristry, so I asked my friend Therese, a professional florist, to show how to create three different arrangements. I've also shown you how to create small winter posies.

Before you buy your flowers consider the colours and think about the setting. Are you creating the bouquet for a special occasion? Look out for colours and shapes that sit well together, depending on the season and what's available to you, and take into account the vessel that your arrangement will sit in. For the largest display we used a vintage cast-iron garden urn, approximately 30cm (12in) tall. You could use a large ceramic jug, vase or clear glass pickle jar like the ones shown left.

After choosing your flowers and foliage spread them out on a table to make it easier when selecting the individual pieces.

I always have a pair of secateurs or scissors to hand, and depending on the arrangement, floristry wire or garden twine and florists' oasis or a small jar or another container to place inside the vase.

In this next section we show you how to create different looks: a large arrangement in an antique garden urn, a medium-sized display in a glass vase, a hand-tied bouquet, and winter posies. These can be adapted to any combination of seasonal flowers and foliage.

A Statement Piece Display

We used a selection of seasonal flowers and leaves ranging in colour from dark clarets through to blues and pale greens for accents, with paler tones of soft pink and cream. These included burgundy alstroemeria and astrantia, blue delphiniums and hyacinths, soft green *Fritillaria* 'Ivory Bells', eucalyptus, viburnum and rose-tinted cow parsley.

Start with a statement piece of foliage in the urn. Trim away any leaves that will sit below the water line as these will decay and limit the longevity of your display.

Let tendrils flow and spill over the sides, keeping the flowers natural and organic.

Form the main frame of the display by adding height in the centre and width on both sides. Start to add in your colour palette with the blues, greens and clarets.

Add piece by piece to build the silhouette. Use the green fritillary and blue delphiniums to balance out the colour interest.

Periodically walk round your display to check for gaps and add in any extra pieces for weight. Use fillers such as the cow parsley and foliage to fill any spaces. The finished arrangement, left, has a good mix of colour and height. See how the colours are balanced throughout: the pale pinks are spread evenly around the top and middle, with darker shades through the centre. The delphiniums provide pops of blue across the arrangement and the light green fritillary takes the eye diagonally across the display, from top left to bottom right. The astrantia is added, top right, for tone and shape.

Once you're happy, top up the urn with water if needed.

A Medium-sized Arrangement

For this bouquet we used protea flowers, long- and round-leaved eucalyptus, rosemary, white stocks, creamy double-crown daffodils and pale pink snapdragons all in a tall glass vase. You may like to try other vibrant foliage such as olive and bay mixed with smoky red spike amaranthus.

Start with the different shades of green foliage for depth and tone, then add the cream double daffodils. Continue turning the arrangement in your hands or vase to see the arrangement from all angles.

Build your display piece by piece adding more depth and colour as you go, in this case the pink snapdragons and protea. Keep it natural-looking by leaving longer pieces like the rosemary and eucalyptus to twist and flow.

Add in the rest of the stocks, foliage fillers and eucalyptus and check that your display has an even balance throughout. When you're happy with the results top the vase up with water from a bottle or jug.

A Hand-tied Bouquet

What you need

A pair of secateurs or scissors
Ribbon (We used 1.5m/5ft of vintage French lace)
A gift card (optional)
Floristry wire or garden twine
A selection of flowers and leaves

For this bouquet we used a selection of seasonal spring flowers including deep purple stocks, plum-coloured tulips, dark inky hyacinths and two types of eucalyptus: a red-tinged narrow leaf and a round-leaf.

Once you've chosen your selection, allow the shape of the flowers and leaves to form the feel of the arrangement. Don't worry about the varying lengths of stems whilst you're putting the flowers together – you'll cut these with secateurs once it's finished.

Continue to play with height as you go, to form a good shape, and twist the bouquet to see it from all angles. When you're happy with the result trim away any unwanted leaves to make way for the string.

Secure the bouquet with floristry wire or string and trim the ends of the stems.

Add ribbon or lace to cover the wire, and a small card if the flowers are intended as a gift.

Winter Posies

For the winter posy overleaf I used white hellebores, eucalyptus, a tendril of ivy, thistle-like blue sea holly and, for contrast, I added a velvety blackberry-coloured scabious, sometimes known as the pincushion flower because of its pin-like stamens. You can, of course, use any combination of seasonal flowers, bought or gathered.

Black and blue anise-scented sage makes a pretty cold-season posy, especially if tied with graceful hellebores, myrtle, white veronica and pale, dusty eucalyptus. Other more unusual arrangements could include foraged bracken, tendrils of rose briar, peppermint, and the striking monochrome of white black-eyed anemones.

For larger, more dramatic bouquets striped amaryllis, with shots of gold and cream, winter camellias and white or the Marbella pink- and champagne-coloured poinsettias all look beautifully festive.

If you're using foraged and fallen twigs, leaves or berries, look for colours and shapes that sit well together.

Once you've selected your flowers and foliage, allow their shape to form the flow of the arrangement.

I often start by putting the flowers in a container to experiment with the silhouette and shape, adding or taking away, as I go. Here I used a 3cm (1in) block of floristss oasis foam in the bottom of an oversized cup to stick the stems in place. You may prefer to pick up one stem at a time and shape the arrangement organically in your hands. Either way, play with different heights so that the shape of your arrangement forms an interesting flow and creates an overall shape that you are happy with. Let the flowers speak for themselves, keep it natural.

Dried maize grass displayed on a salvaged oversize baking tray.

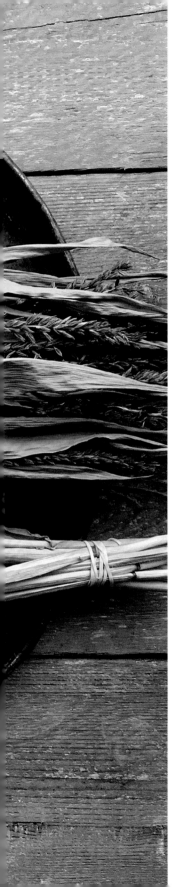

DRYING FLOWERS

I like to decorate the shop with dried flower,s using the last of
the season's hydrangeas. I've experimented with the large purple
Velvet Noir hydrangeas and the 'Glory Blue' variety, shown above.
As the flower heads start to fade just past their best, pour the water
away and leave in the vase to dry until the florets start to crisp;
or tie the stems with a length of string and hang upside down to
dry out completely. You can also dry poppy heads, eucalyptus and
grasses in the same ways.

Sourcebook

FLOWERS & PLANTS

Columbia Road Flower Market, London E2 7RG
Every Sunday 8am–4.30pm

Rebel Rebel
Mare St Market, 117 Mare Street, London, E8 4RU
www.rebelrebel.co.uk

Flower Warehouse
517A Cambridge Heath Rd
020 7729 4444

Conservatory Archives
493–495 Hackney Rd
www.conservatoryarchives.co.uk

GLASSWARE & HOMEWARES

ABC Carpet and Home
A real gem with everything for the home
and more
Manhattan Flagship
888 Broadway
New York, NY 10003

Anthropologie
Nationwide
www.anthropologie.com

East of Earl Candles
5A Gransden Ave, London E8 3QA
www.earlofeastlondon.com

Karin Hossack Pottery
www.etsy.com/uk/shop/KCHossackPottery

Mason & Painter
67 Columbia Rd, London E2 7RG
www.masonandpainter.co.uk

Milagros
61 Columbia Rd, London E2 7RG
www.milagros.co.uk

Nkuku
Brockhills Barns, Harbertonford TQ9 7PS and online
www.nkuku.com

Petersham Nurseries
Vintage and vintage inspired homewares and florists
27–31 King St, Covent Garden
London WC2E 8JB

Vintage Heaven
82 Columbia Rd, London E2 7QB

LINENS & RIBBONS

Liberty
Regent Street, London W1B 5AH
www.libertylondon.com

PAINT, DECORATING & SURFACE SUPPLIES

Leyland
www.leylandtrade.com

Surface Matter
29 Westgate St, London E8 3RL
www.surfacematter.co.uk

POSTCARDS, PRINTS & STATIONERY

Deyrolle
46 Rue du Bac, 75007 Paris, France
www.deyrolle.com

John Derian
6 East Second Street between 2nd Avenue and the
Bowery
New York, NY 10003
www.johnderian.com

National Gallery
Trafalgar Square, London, WC2N 5DN
www.nationalgallery.org.uk

Tate Gallery
Tate Modern, Bankside, London SE1 9TG
www.tate.org.uk

V&A Museum
Cromwell Rd, Knightsbridge, London SW7 2RL
www.vam.ac.uk

SUPPLIES

Pavilion Bakery
18 Broadway Market, London E8 4QJ
www.pavilionbakery.com

VINTAGE MARKETS & ANTIQUE FAIRS

Before heading out please check individual websites
for upcoming fairs and events

UK NORTH

Newark & Nottinghamshire Showground, Drove Lane,
Newark NG24 2NY
www.iacf.co.uk/newark

Sheffield Antique Quarter
To the south of the city, along the A621 and
surrounding roads
www.sheffieldantiquesquarter.co.uk

UK SOUTH

Old Spitalfields Market
16 Horner Square
London, E1 6EW
www.oldspitalfieldsmarket.com/events/antiques-
market

Kempton Antiques Market
Kempton Park, Staines Rd E, Sunbury-on-Thames
TW16 5AQ
www.sunburyantiques.com

FRANCE

Lille
La Grande Braderie de Lille, takes place on the streets
of city centre
https://en.lilletourism.com/lille-flea-market-1.html

Amiens
La Grande Réderie d'Amiens, takes place every April
and October on the streets in the centre of town
www.grande-rederie-amiens.com

USA

Brooklyn Flea
www.brooklynflea.com
Saturdays
241 37th St., Brooklyn, NY

Brooklyn Flea DUMBO
Sundays
Manhattan Bridge Archway, 80 Pearl St., NY

Brimfield Outdoor Antique Shows
Route 20, Brimfield, MA
www.brimfieldshow.com

Alameda Point Antiques Faire
Runway 7/25 Alameda Point
Alameda, California 94501
www.alamedapointantiquesfaire.com

Thanks

Thank you to Jo and Gail at Pimpernel Press for giving me this opportunity and especially to Anna for her patience, words of encouragement and editing. Thanks also to Becky for a sterling job on the design. Thank you to Adam at Sir John Soane's Museum for suggesting that I push ahead with what was initially just an idea and a collection of photographs. Huge thanks to my daughter Marni for putting up with me whilst I worked on the book and forgot basic things like mealtimes. Thanks to William for the very generous loan of a camera and to all the homeowner friends who allowed me to run riot through their flats, houses and gardens.

I'd also like to thank the following people for their generosity of spirit and helpfulness: Carl, Mick, Sylvia, Denise, Paul and Jack and the many stall-holders at Columbia Road Flower Market. To Rebel Rebel flowers for superb flowers, great tips and service with a smile. To Jin at Conservatory Archives, Alexandra at Aesme Flowers and John Kelly at the Barbican Centre. Huge thanks to floral designer and friend Therese Johansson and to Dvora. Also to Penny Wincer for the photographs of flower arrangements on pages 152–165. To Françoize for her advice and friendship and to my Dad and sister for introducing me to Sheffield's antique quarter. And lastly, but by no means least, a huge thank you to Tim Painter, an amazing friend and my business partner at Mason & Painter.

PHOTO CREDITS:
All photography Michelle Mason except
Aesme Flowers p.17
Carol Morley p.134
Paul Vowles p.127
Penny Wincer pp.152–165

LOCATION CREDITS:
Barbican Centre, London
Anthropologie, Spitalfields, London
London Fields, Hackney
Victoria Park, Tower Hamlets
Haggerston Community Orchard, Hackney
Martello Hall, 137 Mare St, London E8 3RH
Conservatory Archives, 493–495 Hackney
Road, London E2 9ED